LDS DOCTRINE AND COVENANTS STUDY GUIDE

Understand the Revelations
with Daily Commentary and Insights

GRAPEVINE BOOKS

Published by
GRAPEVINE BOOKS

www.grapevinebooks.com
email: contact@grapevinebooks.com

Ordering Information:
Quantity sales: Special discounts are available on quantity purchases by corporations, associations, and others.
For details, reach out to the publisher.

First published by Grapevine Books, 2025

CONTENTS

INTRODUCTION

How to Use This Study Guide

Welcome. Whether you are a lifelong member of The Church of Jesus Christ of Latter-day Saints or exploring the Doctrine and Covenants for the first time, this guide is designed to help you deepen your understanding, strengthen your testimony, and apply gospel principles to daily life. The Doctrine and Covenants is unlike any other book of scripture. It is a compilation of modern-day revelations, given in our dispensation, and it speaks directly to the needs and challenges we face today. This guide helps you navigate it with clarity and purpose.

This study guide combines three powerful learning approaches: weekly organization, historical and spiritual context, and personal application. Each part of the book is carefully crafted to help you not only study the scriptures, but also experience them in a way that invites the Spirit and supports personal growth. Whether you're a youth, adult, parent, teacher, or seminary student, you'll find helpful tools in these pages.

How the Guide Is Structured

This book is divided into four main parts, plus an introduction and resource section. You'll begin with foundational chapters that explain key gospel principles, introduce the Doctrine and Covenants, and provide background on figures like Joseph Smith and other early leaders. This gives you a solid footing before diving into the weekly readings.

The heart of this guide is Part 2, which follows a weekly format based on a Big Picture/Little Picture structure. Each week includes a breakdown of the assigned sections, highlights from Church history, and key doctrines. The Big Picture gives you a fast overview with important people, locations, spiritual themes, and maps so you understand the larger purpose. The Little Picture walks you through the actual verses with commentary and reminders of what to watch for.

Seven Spiritual Guiding Questions

Each week also includes seven carefully written questions to help you reflect and apply the scriptures to your own life. These questions are meant to spark inspiration, deepen understanding, and prompt you to make meaningful changes. You can use them for personal journaling, family night discussions, or group study. They are especially helpful for teens and young adults who want to connect gospel principles with real-life challenges.

Who This Guide Is For

This study guide is for anyone who wants to grow closer to Jesus Christ through a focused, uplifting approach to scripture. It works for individuals, families, youth groups, and seminary teachers. It's especially helpful for those who may feel overwhelmed by the depth of the Doctrine and Covenants or who need a manageable structure for daily study.

Busy Latter-day Saints will appreciate the clear format and the balance of study and application. Even if you only have a few minutes each day, you can stay on track with the summaries, visual tools, and reflective prompts. If you are following the Come, Follow Me curriculum, this guide fits alongside it, offering deeper context and space for personal insight.

Tips for Getting the Most from This Guide

- Set aside consistent time for study, even if it's just 10–15 minutes a day.

- Use the Big Picture overview first to understand context, then dive into the detailed study.
- Keep a journal and answer the spiritual guiding questions honestly.
- Teach what you learn. Share insights with friends, family, or your seminary class.
- Don't rush. Let the Spirit teach you at your own pace.

A Note on Flexibility

While this guide is organized by weeks, you do not need to stick rigidly to the calendar. If you fall behind or want to spend more time on a particular section, feel free to adjust your pace. The purpose is not just to finish the book but to be changed by the words of Christ, the revelations given to Joseph Smith, and the lessons the Lord is still teaching us today.

The scriptures are alive. As you study with intention and faith, you will see how they apply to your own questions, trials, and decisions. You'll recognize patterns of revelation, hear the voice of the Lord more clearly, and strengthen your testimony of the restored gospel.

We invite you to move forward with faith, study with purpose, and allow this guide to help you learn the scriptures not just with your mind, but with your heart.

Overview of the Doctrine and Covenants and the Restoration

The Doctrine and Covenants is a book of modern revelation given for a modern world. Unlike ancient scriptures, it contains direct words from the Lord to prophets of this dispensation, beginning with Joseph Smith. These revelations were received in response to real questions and real needs, often in urgent and challenging circumstances. As such, the Doctrine and Covenants does not follow a single storyline. Instead, it unfolds as a collection of inspired answers, prophetic counsel, and divine instructions that form the spiritual foundation of the Church of Jesus Christ of Latter-day Saints.

The Restoration refers to the process through which Jesus Christ brought back His full gospel, priesthood authority, and Church organization after centuries of apostasy. Central to this movement was Joseph Smith, who, through prayer and obedience, became the Lord's chosen prophet to usher in the dispensation of the fulness of times. The Restoration is not a single event but a series of revelations, callings, translations, and ordinances that continue to unfold today. The Doctrine and Covenants is the living record of that process.

This sacred volume includes revelations on gospel doctrines, Church government, commandments, missionary work, temple ordinances, and the gathering of Israel. It also records the trials, questions, and growth of early Church members, making it both a historical document and a deeply spiritual text. As you study the Doctrine and Covenants, you are stepping into the unfolding Restoration, learning directly from the voice of the Lord and the experiences of the Saints.

How the Big Picture/Little Picture Format Enhances Your Daily Study

Studying the scriptures can feel overwhelming, especially when your time is limited and the text is dense. That's why this guide uses a Big Picture/Little Picture format, to help you quickly gain context and then dive deeper with clarity. The Big Picture gives you a simple overview of each week's assigned sections. You'll learn who the key people are, where events take place, what spiritual themes appear, and why the revelations matter. This approach ensures you never start reading cold or confused. You'll see the historical, doctrinal, and spiritual purpose of each block before you begin.

Once you've seen the Big Picture, the Little Picture takes you through the revelations section by section. Each passage is introduced with background notes, reminders of what's happening, and short explanations to help you focus as you read. This has nothing to do with summarizing the entire text but pointing your attention to the most important ideas, questions, and themes so that your reading becomes purposeful and guided.

The combination of both views allows you to engage your mind and heart. You learn the structure and context, and then you reflect, apply, and respond. With this method, even a short daily session can bring deep inspiration and real spiritual progress. Whether you're a youth, adult, teacher, or parent, the Big Picture/Little Picture format will help you stay grounded in the gospel while drawing personal meaning from every page of scripture.

Part 1
Foundations of Faith and Scripture

The Book of Mormon: Learning from Scripture in Latter-day Saint Life

Though this guide focuses on the Doctrine and Covenants, a spiritually complete study includes the Book of Mormon. These two books are companions in the Restoration, testifying of the same Savior and divine plan. When studied together, they offer greater clarity, depth, and power. The Book of Mormon gives voice to ancient prophets who foresaw our day, while the Doctrine and Covenants shows how Christ directs His modern Church. One gives timeless truth. The other brings it into the present.

The Book of Mormon is the keystone of our religion. It testifies of Jesus Christ and teaches core gospel doctrines: faith, repentance, baptism, the gift of the Holy Ghost, and enduring to the end. These same principles echo through the Doctrine and Covenants in the context of a Church being restored under living prophets. Side by side, these books show that the Lord is consistent in every dispensation.

Scripture is not just for information; it's for transformation. The Book of Mormon teaches through narrative and vision. The Doctrine and Covenants builds on that with direct guidance from the Savior. Together, they shape our study, inform our curriculum, and provide daily spiritual strength for individuals and families.

Cross-referencing these books enhances understanding. 2 Nephi 31 explains the doctrine of Christ; Section 20 echoes it as foundational to the restored Church. Section 76 expands our understanding of eternal life, aligning with Alma's and Mosiah's teachings. These parallels remind us that the gospel is one eternal truth, revealed through different voices in different times.

Regular scripture study builds spiritual awareness. Patterns emerge: how the Lord speaks, how people respond, how faith is rewarded. Youth and adults are encouraged to read daily not out of obligation, but to build testimony and draw nearer to God. In seminary, at home, or in quiet reflection, these scriptures offer answers, guidance, and peace.

Prophets in the Book of Mormon modeled how to seek revelation. Nephi, Alma and Enos all asked in faith and received. Joseph Smith followed the same pattern. His First Vision came after reading James 1:5 and praying sincerely. That spirit of inquiry continues in the Doctrine and Covenants, where questions led to revelation. We are invited to follow their example.

Studying scripture means asking, pondering, and applying. This guide encourages all three. As you ask meaningful questions and act on the answers, the scriptures become living messages, personal, relevant, and powerful. The Book of Mormon teaches truth. The Doctrine and Covenants teaches how to live it.

The Lord invites us to search the scriptures diligently. As you study both books together, you will feel the Spirit confirming their truth and experience revelation in your own life. You will come to know the voice of the Lord, and that is where discipleship begins.

Joseph Smith and the Birth of Modern Revelation

To understand the Doctrine and Covenants, you must understand Joseph Smith's role. He was not just a church founder, but a prophet called by God to restore the gospel in its fullness. Through him, the Lord reestablished His Church and opened the final dispensation, the fulness of times. Joseph's life is the gateway to understanding modern revelation.

Raised in humble circumstances with little education, Joseph had a sincere hunger for truth. At age 14, confused by religious division, he read James 1:5 and prayed. In answer, he saw God the Father and Jesus Christ. This First Vision affirmed that the heavens are open and that God still speaks.

Over the next two decades, Joseph received numerous revelations, clear, direct communication from the Lord. They came through visions, the voice of the Spirit, and in response to real questions. Some occurred in prayer, others in meetings or during trials. These revelations addressed practical needs like how to organize the Church, prepare for challenges, preach the gospel, and live faithfully.

The Doctrine and Covenants records these sacred messages. Unlike a traditional narrative, it is a collection of divine instructions. It reveals priesthood authority, temple worship, Church governance, missionary work, and more. Each section reflects the Lord's will for real people facing real challenges.

Joseph was not perfect. The Lord corrected and instructed him, often directly. This transparency shows us that prophets are teachable, not flawless. Joseph's humility and willingness to act in faith make him deeply relatable. His life teaches that revelation comes to those who seek it sincerely.

One of Joseph's most powerful traits was his courage to ask. He didn't pretend to know everything. He sought the Lord in prayer, trusted in His timing, and followed His answers. This is how modern revelation works: through questions, effort, and trust.

Many of the revelations Joseph received were for the entire Church, but others were deeply personal, offering comfort, guidance, and direction to individuals. That pattern remains today. The Lord speaks to His prophets on behalf of the Church, and to each of us in our personal lives.

Through Joseph, the Restoration unfolded. The Book of Mormon was translated, the priesthood restored, temples revealed, and the Church organized. Each milestone required revelation and each one required Joseph to move forward in faith, even without knowing the full picture.

Joseph Smith's life stands as a witness that God is not silent. Revelation continues through living prophets and personal inspiration. The Doctrine and Covenants is a record of that truth. It invites us to seek the Lord's voice in our own lives, to follow it, and to help build the kingdom of God.

What Is Revelation? Learning to Hear the Voice of Jesus Christ

Revelation is at the core of the Doctrine and Covenants. Every section is a record of the Lord responding to questions, needs, or crises. They are not ancient voices, but modern answers for modern people. Just as God guided the early Saints, He continues to speak today. Like Joseph Smith, we can learn to recognize and follow personal revelation in our lives.

Joseph didn't just pray; he expected answers. That faith made him a prophet, but his example is meant for all of us. Revelation came to him through visions, dreams, impressions, angelic visits, and direct communication. It came in prayer, during meetings, and in response to others' questions. God met him where he was, and He meets us where we are.

Section 6 teaches that God speaks to both the mind and the heart. Oliver Cowdery was told revelation had already come. He just hadn't recognized it. That's often true for us. Revelation may feel like peace, clarity, a warm feeling, or a sudden prompting. Sometimes it's bold and urgent. Often, it unfolds gradually as we act in faith.

The Lord invites us to ask but also to ponder, study, and wait. Revelation doesn't come on demand. It comes when we are prepared to receive it. Section 8 emphasizes that personal revelation involves both our spirit and our intellect. It is sacred, practical, and ongoing.

This guide is designed to help you learn that pattern. Each weekly study includes Seven Spiritual Guiding Questions to help you listen and act. As you apply what you learn, your ability to receive revelation grows. The way the Spirit speaks to you may be unique, but the Lord always keeps His promise: He will guide you.

Revelation is not just about getting answers; it's about building a relationship with Jesus Christ. As you seek His voice, you will feel His presence more deeply. His guidance will help you make choices, find comfort, and serve others. Sometimes His answers come through people. Sometimes they follow a leap of faith.

Through the Doctrine and Covenants, we see how the Lord led the early Saints in matters spiritual and practical, like organizing the Church, sending missionaries, correcting errors, and revealing truth. That same divine help is available to us today. Whether we seek guidance in school, family, faith, or purpose, revelation lights the way.

As you study, write down your thoughts and impressions. Ask what the Lord would have you learn and then act. Revelation grows stronger when we respond to it. Like a muscle, it strengthens with use. And with time, you'll gain greater confidence in hearing the Lord's voice.

The Lord is speaking. Are we listening? Use this time to tune your heart. The Doctrine and Covenants is an invitation to hear Him today.

The Restoration:
A Modern Gospel Movement for the Church

The Restoration is one of history's most important spiritual events and an ongoing movement. It began with a prayer by 14-year-old Joseph Smith, who wanted to know which church was true. In response, God the Father and Jesus Christ appeared to him in the First Vision. That event opened the heavens and began the final dispensation.

Step by step, the Restoration unfolded. The Book of Mormon was translated and published in 1830. The Aaronic and Melchizedek Priesthoods were restored by angels, enabling sacred ordinances like baptism and the gift of the Holy Ghost to return. The Church of Jesus Christ of Latter-day Saints was officially organized by revelation on April 6, 1830.

From there, the Lord continued to reveal truth: the nature of God, the plan of salvation, temple ordinances, eternal families, missionary work, and more. The Restoration not only restored the Church's structure but also restored rich doctrine that shapes how we understand life, purpose, and eternity.

The Doctrine and Covenants stands as the official record of this unfolding Restoration. It contains modern revelations, words from Jesus Christ to real people in real situations. These revelations guide the Church in organization, repentance, service, and preparation for the Second Coming.

One of the Restoration's greatest gifts is participation. Every member is a contributor, not just a receiver. We are asked to study, teach, serve, and testify. In doing so, we help move the Lord's work forward. The Restoration is still happening through us.

Ongoing revelation is central to this work. The Lord continues to guide His Church through living prophets. He didn't reveal everything all at once. Through prophets and apostles, He speaks today just as He did anciently. When they speak by the Holy Ghost, it is as if the Lord Himself were speaking.

For families, the Restoration brought back eternal truths about divine roles, covenants, and sacred ordinances. For youth, it offers purpose and identity in a confusing world. For all of us, it brings assurance that we belong to Christ's Church.

As you study the Doctrine and Covenants, you are witnessing the Restoration in motion. Each section is part of the divine blueprint. And it is not just Church history; it is personal. These revelations answer your questions, deepen your faith, and draw you closer to Christ.

The Restoration is our present and future. It is a movement of light and power. By studying, living, and sharing these truths, you help carry that movement forward. The Restoration continues every time someone opens their heart to the Lord.

Commandments, Context, and Inspired Living

One of the central messages in the Doctrine and Covenants is the Lord's invitation to keep His commandments not as restrictions, but as loving guidance meant for our happiness, protection, and spiritual growth. These commandments, given through revelation, were responses to real questions and needs. They came during times of uncertainty and transition, showing that the Lord speaks to His people in timely and personal ways.

Understanding the context behind these revelations helps us apply them today. For example, the Word of Wisdom, originally introduced as counsel, became a commandment through prophetic guidance. Tithing was revealed when the Church faced financial difficulty, providing both a principle of faith and a way to support the Lord's work. Similar patterns exist in commandments related to missionary service, Sabbath observance, and moral conduct. Each principle, though revealed long ago, carries lasting relevance and power.

When we obey with sincere intent, commandments become more than checklists. They become part of our covenant relationship with God. They bring the Holy Ghost into our lives, strengthen faith in Jesus Christ, and lead to greater personal revelation. Obedience builds spiritual confidence and prepares us to receive further light.

Inspired living means choosing to follow the Savior out of love, not fear. As we keep commandments, we are shaped into disciples. We develop humility, trust, and strength to stand firm in a changing world. Families, youth, and individuals find peace, confidence, and clarity as they live by divine principles.

The Doctrine and Covenants teaches that commandments are part of the covenant path, leading us to temple covenants, priesthood service, and lifelong discipleship. As you study, reflect on both the "what" and the "why" behind the Lord's instructions. With understanding, obedience becomes a joyful expression of love and faith.

Commandments are not burdens. They are blessings from a loving Father who wants us to become like His Son. When we choose to follow them with intention, we choose a life filled with purpose, strength, and eternal promise.

The Power of Testimony and Personal Growth

A testimony is more than a belief. It is a spiritual witness that comes from the Holy Ghost, confirming that something is true. In the context of the Doctrine and Covenants, we learn that testimony is not only essential for conversion but also for endurance and growth. The early Saints faced trials, sacrifices, and uncertainty, yet they moved forward because they knew the gospel was true. Their testimonies gave them strength. Ours can do the same.

Building a testimony begins with desire. Alma taught that even a desire to believe can grow into faith. As we study scripture, pray with intent, and keep the commandments, the Holy Ghost confirms truth to our hearts and minds. This confirmation is quiet but powerful. It brings peace, clarity, and confidence. The Doctrine and Covenants invites us to seek personal revelation, and as we do, our testimony becomes deeply rooted.

Testimony leads to action. When we know that Jesus Christ lives, that Joseph Smith was a prophet, and that the Church is true, we naturally want to serve, share, and live in harmony with those truths. A testimony becomes a guide in our decisions, a comfort in times of doubt, and a motivator when challenges arise. It fuels personal growth by connecting us to God's plan.

Personal growth is not about perfection. It is about progress. The Lord teaches line upon line, and our understanding increases over time. The revelations in the Doctrine and Covenants often addressed Saints who were learning, repenting, and trying again. That pattern applies to us. As our testimonies grow, so does our capacity to change, forgive, endure, and lead.

Each time you bear your testimony, live your beliefs, or act on what the Spirit teaches you, your spiritual foundation becomes stronger. Through that process, you draw closer to Jesus Christ and become more like Him. The journey of personal growth is lifelong, and your testimony is what carries you forward. It is both the anchor that holds you firm and the light that helps you move ahead. Keep nurturing it, and it will grow into a lifelong source of power and peace.

Part 2
Weekly Study Guides, Section Summaries & Journal Prompts

Week 1

Theme: The Voice of the Lord and the Call to Repentance

BIG PICTURE

Revelations Covered: Doctrine and Covenants Sections 1–5

Historical Period: November 1828 – March 1829

This first week of study introduces the tone and purpose of the Doctrine and Covenants. It begins not with the earliest revelation chronologically but with the Lord's own preface to the book. In it, the Lord declares that He is speaking again to the world, calling all people to repentance, and preparing the way for His Second Coming. These five sections show us how the Lord works through imperfect people, offers correction with mercy, and invites all to participate in His work.

These early revelations were given to individuals who were either close to Joseph Smith or seeking to understand their place in the Restoration. In these sections, we see the Lord rebuking, calling, comforting, and directing. The voice we hear is not just historical—it is living, personal, and direct.

Key People:

- **Joseph Smith Jr.** – Called by the Lord to be a prophet, seer, and translator. He is learning to discern the Lord's voice while facing public and private pressure.
- **Martin Harris** – A supporter of the translation project who struggles with doubts. His role is challenged after the loss of the 116 pages.
- **Joseph Smith Sr.** – Joseph's father, a man of faith and support, called by revelation to begin his service.
- **Oliver Cowdery** (briefly mentioned here) – Will be introduced more fully in Week 2.

Key Locations:

- **Harmony, Pennsylvania** – Where Joseph and Emma lived during much of the Book of Mormon translation process. Many of these early revelations were received here.
- **Manchester, New York** – Home of the Smith family and where early discussions with Martin Harris took place.

Contextual Insight:

At this stage, the Church has not yet been formally organized. Joseph is facing intense pressure following the loss of the Book of Mormon manuscript. These revelations reflect both divine rebuke and divine reassurance. The Lord is preparing His prophet for greater responsibilities, and He is setting the spiritual tone for the Restoration.

Spiritual Themes:

- The Lord's voice in the last days
- Repentance and spiritual preparation
- The reality of divine correction
- The call to serve in the Lord's work
- The difference between seeking signs and acting in faith
- The rising importance of witnesses to the Book of Mormon

SPIRITUAL CONTEXT AND OVERVIEW OF THE SECTIONS

Section 1 – The Lord's Preface to the Doctrine and Covenants

This section, although received later, is placed first because it serves as the Lord's personal introduction to the entire Doctrine and Covenants. It is not the voice of Joseph Smith—it is the voice of Jesus Christ addressing the world in the latter days. The Lord warns of coming calamities, calls all to repentance, and declares that He speaks through His chosen servants. This revelation establishes the authority and urgency of modern scripture and affirms that the Restoration is His work, not man's.

Key Concepts:

- The Lord speaks again in our time through revelation
- Repentance is a central requirement for spiritual safety
- God's word will reach every nation and individual
- The Doctrine and Covenants is meant for the entire world

Section 2 – The Promise of Elijah

This brief section is a direct quote of what the angel Moroni repeated to Joseph Smith from the book of Malachi. Though only three verses long, it points to a foundational doctrine of the Restoration: the sealing power and the turning of hearts through temple covenants. It links modern revelation with ancient prophecy and anticipates the restoration of priesthood keys that will bind families for eternity.

Key Concepts:

- The hearts of families must be turned to one another
- Elijah's mission is central to the Restoration
- Family history and temple work are divinely connected
- Prophetic promises are being fulfilled in modern times

Section 3 – The Lord Rebukes and Recommissions Joseph Smith

After Joseph allowed Martin Harris to take the 116-page manuscript, and it was lost, he faced deep sorrow and fear. In this revelation, the Lord lovingly corrects Joseph, reminding him that he must fear God more than man. The Lord reaffirms that His work will go forward, even if His servants fall short. Joseph is told to repent, recommit, and continue his sacred calling.

Key Concepts:

- God's work cannot be frustrated by human mistakes
- Prophetic calling requires obedience and humility
- Mercy is extended even after serious error
- God's trust can be restored through repentance

Section 4 – A Call to Serve Given to Joseph Smith Sr.

This short but beloved section is a revelation to Joseph Smith's father, calling him into the Lord's service. It teaches that the desire to serve is enough to be called and outlines the attributes the Lord seeks in His servants. It remains one of the most quoted missionary texts in the Church.

Key Concepts:

- Service begins with righteous desire
- Spiritual attributes prepare us for effective discipleship
- Every person has a role in the Lord's work
- The field is ready for harvest—now is the time to act

Section 5 – The Lord's Counsel to Martin Harris

Martin Harris requests a revelation for reassurance. The Lord responds by explaining that faith must come before signs. He also references the coming of the Three Witnesses and reminds Martin that testimony is built through obedience, not demands. This section emphasizes trust in divine timing and the sacred role of witnesses.

Key Concepts:

- Revelation is not granted to satisfy doubt
- Testimony is rooted in faith, not proof
- Witnesses are chosen and prepared by the Lord
- Obedience opens the way to spiritual confirmation

LITTLE PICTURE: SECTION-BY-SECTION INSIGHT

Section 1 – The Lord's Preface to the Doctrine and Covenants

This revelation, though received after many others, was placed first in the Doctrine and Covenants because it is the Lord's official introduction to His book of commandments. Speaking directly to all people, the Lord declares that His voice is speaking again in the latter days. He warns of coming judgments and invites everyone to repent and listen to the words of His prophets. This section sets the tone for the entire book—it is bold, urgent, and filled with divine authority.

Before You Read: Ask yourself, "If the Lord were speaking to the entire world today, what would He say?" This section answers that question directly.

Key Verses to Watch:

• Verse 4: "The voice of warning shall be unto all people"

• Verse 14: "And the arm of the Lord shall be revealed"

• Verse 38: "Whether by mine own voice or by the voice of my servants, it is the same"

Core Message: The Lord is calling the world to repent. His voice speaks through living prophets, and His words will not be silenced.

Section 2 – The Promise of Elijah

This short but foundational revelation is a repetition of Moroni's words to Joseph Smith about the prophecy found in Malachi. It introduces the role of Elijah in the Restoration and the importance of family connections across generations. Though only three verses, it opens the door to temple work and the eternal linking of families.

Before You Read: Consider the importance of family in the gospel. How does your faith connect to your ancestors and descendants?

Key Verses to Watch:

• Entire section (all three verses are meaningful)

Core Message: The priesthood keys of Elijah are returning. The work of sealing families across generations is central to the Restoration.

Section 3 – The Lord Corrects and Reassures Joseph Smith

After the 116 manuscript pages were lost, Joseph felt discouraged and uncertain. This revelation from the Lord corrects Joseph for fearing man more than God, but it also offers reassurance. Joseph is told to repent and continue the work. The Lord makes it clear that His purposes will not be frustrated, even by mistakes.

Before You Read: Think of a time you made a mistake and feared the consequences. How did the Lord show you mercy while helping you learn?

Key Verses to Watch:

• Verse 3: "The works, and the designs, and the purposes of God cannot be frustrated"

• Verse 10: "But remember, God is merciful; therefore, repent"

Core Message: God's work continues in spite of human weakness. When we repent, the Lord restores our calling and confidence.

Section 4 – A Call to Serve for Joseph Smith Sr.

This revelation is addressed to Joseph's father, who desired to serve in the Lord's work. It teaches that anyone with a desire to serve is called. The Lord lists qualities needed for discipleship and emphasizes that the field is ready for harvest. This section is often shared with missionaries and new converts.

Before You Read: Reflect on your desire to serve. What does it mean to be "called" even before you feel ready?

Key Verses to Watch:

• Verse 2: "Serve him with all your heart, might, mind and strength"

• Verse 5–6: Attributes the Lord requires in His servants

Core Message: The Lord calls those who are willing. Service is about commitment and Christlike attributes, not perfection.

Section 5 – The Lord's Instructions to Martin Harris

Martin Harris sought a revelation to strengthen his resolve and confirm his place in the work. The Lord answers, but also teaches an important lesson—revelation comes through faith, not demand. He speaks of the future Three Witnesses and warns Martin to humble himself and obey. Testimony, the Lord says, is built through obedience, not signs.

Before You Read: Ask yourself whether you sometimes seek proof before believing. What does it mean to walk by faith?

Key Verses to Watch:

• Verse 7: "Behold, if they will not believe my words, they would not believe you, my servant Joseph"

• Verse 24: "And if you do this, behold I grant unto you eternal life"

Core Message: Faith precedes witness. The Lord gives assurance to the humble and calls His servants to act in faith before confirmation comes.

SPIRITUAL GUIDING QUESTIONS

1. **What does it mean to you personally that the Lord's voice is heard again in our time?**
2. Consider how this truth affects your relationship with scripture, prophets, and personal prayer.
3. **Why do you think the Lord begins the Doctrine and Covenants with a voice of warning instead of comfort?**
4. How does this approach reflect His love and concern for the world?
5. **In Section 3, how does the Lord balance correction with mercy when addressing Joseph Smith?**
6. What can you learn from this as you face your own mistakes?
7. **What invitation is the Lord giving you through these five sections?**
8. What action will you take this week based on what you have read?

JOURNAL PROMPTS

- **Write about a time you received a spiritual correction that helped you grow.**
- How did it change your direction or deepen your understanding?
- **Choose one attribute from Section 4 and record how you will practice it this week.**
- For example, if you choose diligence, describe what that looks like in your daily study or family life.
- **Record your thoughts on what it means to hear the voice of the Lord in modern times.**
- How has your study this week helped you recognize revelation more clearly?

APPLICATION FOR YOUTH AND ADULTS

For Youth:

Read Section 4 and highlight the traits the Lord lists. Choose one and make it your "focus trait" this week. Tell a parent, teacher, or friend what you picked, and ask them to help you notice when you are practicing it. Use this as part of your Come, Follow Me or seminary journal.

For Adults:

Reflect on the Lord's rebuke in Section 3 and how it applies to your spiritual responsibility. Is there something the Lord has asked you to do that you have delayed or set aside? How can you act in faith, even when it feels difficult? Review your personal or family scripture study plan and ask the Lord how to improve it.

CLOSING THOUGHTS FOR WEEK 1

The first five sections of the Doctrine and Covenants set a powerful spiritual tone for your study. You have encountered the direct voice of Jesus Christ, calling His people to repentance, inviting them to serve, correcting them with love, and preparing them for what lies ahead. These revelations are not just history—they are instruction for your life right now.

As you continue your study, carry forward what you've learned about obedience, humility, and the Lord's mercy. This is the beginning of a journey of spiritual growth. The Lord is calling, and He is still speaking. Keep listening. Keep acting. Keep growing.

Week 2

Theme: Receiving Personal Revelation and the Role of the Holy Ghost

BIG PICTURE

Revelations Covered: Doctrine and Covenants Sections 6–9

Historical Period: April 1829

This week's study explores how the Lord teaches us to recognize and receive revelation. Through His words to Joseph Smith and Oliver Cowdery, we learn about the voice of the Spirit, the workings of the heart and mind, and the importance of humility and faith in the revelatory process. These sections are among the most personal and instructive in the entire Doctrine and Covenants, offering a clear pattern for how revelation works in the lives of the faithful.

At this point in Church history, Oliver Cowdery had just arrived to assist Joseph as a scribe in the translation of the Book of Mormon. Though new to the process, Oliver had already received personal revelation prompting him to travel to Harmony, Pennsylvania. The Lord responds to his faith by giving him instruction through these four sections. We also see the spiritual companionship forming between Joseph and Oliver, as both men rely on divine guidance to fulfill their sacred responsibilities.

The Lord's tone in these revelations is deeply reassuring. He reminds both Joseph and Oliver that He knows their thoughts, their prayers, and their efforts. These chapters reveal that the Lord is close to those who seek Him. We see the sacred nature of spiritual gifts, the role of the Holy Ghost, and the Lord's expectations for those who ask for His help. While the revelations contain instructions specifically for Joseph and Oliver, they also model how anyone can seek and receive answers from God.

Key People:

- **Joseph Smith Jr.** – Receiving guidance and learning how to teach Oliver about spiritual gifts and the work of translation.
- **Oliver Cowdery** – Newly arrived as Joseph's scribe; full of faith and questions, seeking his own spiritual confirmation.

Key Locations:

- **Harmony, Pennsylvania** – The translation of the Book of Mormon is in progress here, and it is where these revelations are received.

Spiritual Themes:

- Revelation comes by faith, not force
- The Lord speaks to both the mind and the heart
- Peace is a witness of truth
- The Holy Ghost is the key to personal guidance

- Asking, trusting, and acting are essential parts of the revelatory process
- Revelation is given according to spiritual preparation

SPIRITUAL CONTEXT AND OVERVIEW OF THE SECTIONS

Section 6 – Revelation to Oliver Cowdery

Oliver has arrived and begun assisting with the translation. He is full of faith but still new to the revelatory process. The Lord tells him that He already spoke peace to his mind and reminds him that this quiet assurance was revelation. Oliver is promised further gifts and encouraged to continue in the work with patience and faith.

Key Concepts:

- Revelation is already occurring—we must learn to recognize it
- The Lord honors righteous desires
- Personal spiritual impressions are sacred and valid
- Peace is a powerful form of confirmation

Section 7 – A Visionary Revelation About John the Beloved

Joseph and Oliver wonder whether John the Beloved died or was allowed to remain on earth. Rather than speculate, they ask the Lord. In response, they receive a translated parchment that clarifies John's desire and the Lord's promise to him. This revelation shows that doctrinal questions can be answered through revelation and confirms that ancient promises are still active.

Key Concepts:

- The Lord answers sincere questions of doctrine
- Ancient records still have relevance and power
- Revelation brings clarity and connection between dispensations

Section 8 – Revelation and the Spirit of Revelation

The Lord promises Oliver the spirit of revelation, which will work through both the heart and the mind. This section also references the gift of Aaron, which relates to the power to translate and receive inspired instruction. It emphasizes the active, cooperative nature of revelation.

Key Concepts:

- The Holy Ghost is a revelator
- Mind and heart work together in receiving truth
- Faith is required before confirmation comes
- Spiritual gifts are real and available

Section 9 – Counsel to Oliver About Translation

Oliver had hoped to help with the actual translation of the plates. He is gently corrected here. The Lord tells him that he must study things out in his mind, and then ask for confirmation. Because he did not continue as he began, he lost the opportunity, but not the Lord's trust. He is told to continue as a scribe.

Key Concepts:

- Revelation requires effort, study, and humility
- The Lord corrects with love and instructs for growth
- Each person has a role to fulfill in the Lord's work
- Failure can be part of the learning process

LITTLE PICTURE: SECTION-BY-SECTION INSIGHT

Section 6 – The Lord Speaks Peace to Oliver Cowdery

This revelation is a warm and encouraging message to Oliver Cowdery shortly after he begins helping Joseph Smith with the translation. The Lord tells Oliver that He has already been communicating with him through feelings of peace. Oliver is reminded that personal revelation does not always come in dramatic ways. Sometimes, it comes quietly, through spiritual impressions that calm and reassure.

Before You Read: Think of a time when you felt peace while making a decision. That peace was likely the Spirit confirming truth to you. The Lord teaches Oliver—and us—that those moments are real and sacred.

Key Verses to Watch:

- Verse 15: "Did I not speak peace to your mind concerning the matter?"
- Verse 36: "Look unto me in every thought; doubt not, fear not."

Core Message: The Lord is already speaking. Our work is to recognize His voice and trust it.

Section 7 – Revelation About John the Beloved

Joseph and Oliver are discussing a gospel question: did the Apostle John die, or did he remain on the earth? Rather than speculate, they ask the Lord. In response, He provides a translated version of John's own writing, clarifying that John was allowed to remain to bring souls unto Christ. This moment teaches us that doctrinal curiosity, when approached faithfully, can lead to revelation.

Before You Read: Consider that not all revelation is personal. Sometimes it answers questions about doctrine or expands our view of God's work across time.

Key Verses to Watch:

- Entire section (it is short but rich in meaning)

Core Message: Revelation connects past and present. The Lord honors righteous desires and answers faithful inquiry.

Section 8 – The Spirit of Revelation

In this revelation, the Lord tells Oliver that the gift of revelation is available to him through the Holy Ghost. It will come through both the heart and the mind. Oliver is promised the same spirit that guided Moses as he parted the Red Sea. This section contains one of the most quoted teachings about how revelation feels and functions.

Before You Read: Have you ever wondered how to know if something is a prompting? This section gives direct answers.

Key Verses to Watch:

- Verse 2: "Yea, behold, I will tell you in your mind and in your heart…"
- Verse 3: "This is the spirit of revelation."

Core Message: Revelation is real and active. It requires sensitivity, faith, and personal preparation.

Section 9 – Counsel About the Translation Effort

Oliver had hoped to help translate the Book of Mormon. The Lord acknowledges his righteous desire but explains that he did not continue as he began. He is told that revelation requires not only desire but mental effort and patience. The Lord gently redirects Oliver to continue serving as a scribe and reassures him of his value in the work.

Before You Read: Think of a time you tried something and failed or had to change direction. How did the Lord guide you through that?

Key Verses to Watch:

- Verse 8: "You must study it out in your mind…"
- Verse 10: "Be faithful, and yield to no temptation."

Core Message: Revelation is a partnership. The Lord expects us to do our part—to think, prepare, and trust—and He will do His.

SPIRITUAL GUIDING QUESTIONS

1. **Have you ever experienced peace after making a prayerful decision?**
2. How does Section 6 help you recognize that feeling as a form of revelation?
3. **What can you learn from the Lord's reassurance to Oliver Cowdery about trusting quiet impressions?**
4. How might this change your approach to spiritual decision-making?
5. **In Section 7, Joseph and Oliver ask a doctrinal question and receive revelation.**
6. **How can you follow that example when you have questions about the gospel?**
7. **Section 8 teaches that revelation comes to both the mind and the heart.**
8. What does that mean in your daily life? Can you recall a time when that pattern was true for you?
9. **Section 9 corrects Oliver but with love.**
10. How do you respond when the Lord's answer is "not now" or "not this way"? What does faithful obedience look like in those moments?

JOURNAL PROMPTS

1. **Describe a recent situation where you felt unsure about a decision.**
2. What impressions or feelings came as you prayed or studied? Did you notice peace, clarity, or quiet encouragement?
3. **Write about a gospel question you currently have.**
4. What steps can you take to seek a revelatory answer in the same way Joseph and Oliver did?
5. **Reflect on the phrase "study it out in your mind."**
6. What does that look like for you? How can you practice this principle in your scripture study or problem-solving?

APPLICATION FOR YOUTH AND ADULTS

For Youth:

Choose one way this week to act on a prompting, even if it feels small. It might be talking to someone who needs kindness, studying a particular topic in the scriptures, or asking a trusted adult for advice. Keep a short note about how you felt before and after.

For Adults:

Pay attention to how the Lord may already be communicating with you through your thoughts, impressions, and feelings. Set aside five minutes daily to quietly reflect and write down any peaceful thoughts you notice. Use Section 6 as a guide to discern how the Lord "speaks peace" to you.

CLOSING THOUGHTS FOR WEEK 2

These four sections offer a sacred blueprint for learning how to hear the Lord. You are not expected to be perfect in receiving revelation. You are expected to ask, to trust, and to act. The Lord's promise to Oliver is also for you: He knows your thoughts. He has heard your prayers. And He will speak peace to your heart and mind as you seek Him with real intent.

The revelations of this week remind us that the Spirit speaks often and personally. You are capable of receiving divine guidance. As you continue your study, let these truths strengthen your confidence. The gift of revelation is not distant or reserved for a few—it is a living reality for those who are willing to listen.

Week 3

Theme: Calling, Authority, and the Worth of Souls

BIG PICTURE

Revelations Covered: Doctrine and Covenants Sections 10–13

Historical Period: Summer 1828 – May 1829

This week focuses on the Lord's ability to move His work forward, even when His servants falter. These sections address both loss and renewal, beginning with Joseph's repentance following the loss of the 116 manuscript pages. The Lord reaffirms that His purposes will not be frustrated. From there, the revelations move into themes of priesthood authority and missionary preparation.

Joseph and Oliver continue the translation of the Book of Mormon, and their work leads them to ask about baptism and priesthood. In answer, John the Baptist appears and confers the Aaronic Priesthood. This moment is a key event in the Restoration of the gospel and the reestablishment of Christ's authority on earth.

These revelations also highlight the immense value the Lord places on each soul. He teaches that preaching the gospel and inviting others to repent is among the most important work we can do. The language of these sections is bold, urgent, and filled with love. The Lord's mercy is evident, and so is His expectation that those who serve Him must do so with sincerity, humility, and focus.

Key People:

- Joseph Smith Jr. – Repenting, recommitting, and continuing the translation
- Oliver Cowdery – Learning about the priesthood and assisting with the work
- John the Baptist – Appears as a resurrected being to restore the Aaronic Priesthood

Key Locations:

- Harmony, Pennsylvania – Ongoing translation and key revelations
- Susquehanna River – Site of the first baptisms under restored priesthood authority

Spiritual Themes:

- God's work cannot be stopped by human error
- The repentance process is personal and powerful
- Souls are of infinite worth
- Authority must be conferred by God, not assumed
- The Restoration includes the return of ancient priesthood power
- Gospel work is urgent and sacred

SPIRITUAL CONTEXT AND OVERVIEW OF THE SECTIONS

Section 10 – The Lord's Counsel After the Lost Manuscript

This section is given after the loss of the 116 pages. The Lord tells Joseph not to retranslate, as enemies would try to discredit the work. Instead, He reveals that He prepared the plates of Nephi as a backup centuries earlier. The Lord reassures Joseph that his mission is not over and invites him to continue the work with new focus.

Key Concepts:

• God's foreknowledge allows His plan to succeed

• Satan stirs up opposition, but the Lord's work is protected

• Repentance brings renewal

• The Book of Mormon is meant to bring souls to Christ

Section 11 – Revelation to Hyrum Smith

Hyrum desires to preach, but the Lord first instructs him to prepare. He emphasizes the importance of the Spirit, personal study, and righteous living before engaging in public ministry.

Key Concepts:

• A desire to serve is noble, but preparation is essential

• The Spirit must guide our words and actions

• The Lord's work requires patience and obedience

• Personal revelation comes to the spiritually prepared

Section 12 – Revelation to Joseph Knight Sr.

Joseph Knight wants to assist in the Lord's work. Like Hyrum, he is told that the field is ready and that service is available to all who are humble and full of love.

Key Concepts:

• Humility and charity are qualifications for service

• The Lord invites all to participate in His work

• Every disciple has a role to play in the Restoration

Section 13 – The Restoration of the Aaronic Priesthood

John the Baptist appears to Joseph and Oliver, laying his hands on them and conferring priesthood authority. This section contains the exact words he spoke. It is short but monumental, marking the return of divine power to baptize and administer ordinances.

Key Concepts:

• Priesthood power is given by authorized messengers

• The Aaronic Priesthood includes the keys of baptism and repentance

• The Restoration is literal and ongoing

• Authority from God is essential for gospel ordinances

LITTLE PICTURE: SECTION-BY-SECTION INSIGHT

Section 10 – The Lord Protects His Work After the Lost Manuscript

This revelation comes after Joseph's deep sorrow and repentance for losing the 116 manuscript pages. The Lord commands Joseph not to retranslate the lost portion, revealing that evil men would try to alter the manuscript and discredit the work. Instead, the Lord instructs Joseph to translate from the plates of Nephi, which were preserved for this very purpose. This section reassures Joseph that God's work is not halted by human error and that the Book of Mormon will still go forth.

Before You Read: Think about a time when you made a mistake but found a new path forward. How did the Lord show you mercy and direction?

Key Verses to Watch:

• Verse 4: "Do not run faster or labor more than you have strength"

• Verse 43: "I will not suffer that they shall destroy my work"

Core Message: The Lord's work cannot be frustrated. Repentance restores trust, and God always has a backup plan.

Section 11 – Counsel to Hyrum Smith About Ministry

Hyrum desires to declare the gospel, but the Lord counsels him to first obtain His word and prepare spiritually. This section emphasizes the power of the Spirit and the importance of patience and study before preaching. Hyrum is promised that if he prepares, the time will come when he will be able to declare the Lord's word with power.

Before You Read: Are there things you want to do for the Lord that require spiritual preparation first?

Key Verses to Watch:

• Verse 12: "Put your trust in that Spirit which leadeth to do good"

• Verse 21: "Seek not to declare my word, but first seek to obtain my word"

Core Message: True service begins with preparation. The Lord's work requires a foundation of personal righteousness.

Section 12 – A Revelation to Joseph Knight Sr. About Service

Joseph Knight Sr., a friend and supporter of Joseph Smith, desires to know how he can help in the Lord's work. The Lord responds by teaching that all who have the desire and who are humble and full of love are called to assist. This short section highlights the inclusive and spiritual nature of discipleship.

Before You Read: Consider what "desire" means in the Lord's eyes. Are you willing to serve, even in small ways?

Key Verses to Watch:

• Verse 3: "Whosoever will thrust in his sickle and reap, the same is called of God"

• Verse 8: "And no one can assist in this work except he shall be humble and full of love"

Core Message: The Lord calls all who are willing and faithful. Your desire to serve is already a sign that the Lord can use you.

Section 13 – The Restoration of the Aaronic Priesthood

This brief but powerful section records the exact words John the Baptist spoke when he appeared to Joseph Smith and Oliver Cowdery and restored the Aaronic Priesthood. This event took place on the banks of the Susquehanna River. With this priesthood came the keys of baptism, repentance, and ministering of angels.

Before You Read: Think about the ordinances you've participated in. What does it mean to know they were performed with restored priesthood authority?

Key Verses to Watch:

• The entire section (it is a single verse)

Core Message: Priesthood authority has been restored to the earth. Ordinances are valid only when performed by that authority, which now operates in the Church of Jesus Christ of Latter-day Saints.

SPIRITUAL GUIDING QUESTIONS

1. **What do you learn from the Lord's handling of the lost manuscript situation in Section 10?**
2. How does this revelation help you when facing personal mistakes or failures?
3. **What qualities does the Lord list in Section 12 as necessary for those assisting in the Restoration?**
4. Which of those attributes do you feel strong in? Which would you like to develop further?
5. **How does the Restoration of the Aaronic Priesthood affect your personal experiences with baptism, the sacrament, or other ordinances?**
6. What feelings or memories come to mind as you reflect on that?
7. **What does this week's study reveal about how the Lord prepares individuals for their roles in His work?**
8. How has He been preparing you?

JOURNAL PROMPTS

• Reflect on a time when you made a mistake and the Lord still helped you move forward.

How does Section 10 comfort or inspire you?

• Write about a desire you have to serve in the Church or help someone spiritually.

How can you begin preparing for that today?

• List the spiritual attributes found in Section 12.

Which one stands out to you and why? Record a goal related to it.

• Record your thoughts about the Restoration of the Aaronic Priesthood.

How does it affect your understanding of baptism and repentance?

APPLICATION FOR YOUTH AND ADULTS

For Youth:

Choose one spiritual attribute from Section 12 and focus on developing it this week. You might try being more loving, patient, or humble in your home or with friends. Keep a short note about what you tried and how it felt.

For Adults:

Take time this week to "obtain the word" by studying a gospel topic deeply. It could be priesthood authority, repentance, or spiritual gifts. Prepare as if you were going to teach it. Then look for a way to share it naturally in a conversation, family night, or Church setting.

CLOSING THOUGHTS FOR WEEK 3

This week's revelations show that the Lord is patient, merciful, and always ready to move His work forward—even when we falter. He corrects with love, invites with purpose, and prepares with precision. The Restoration is not just about the return of doctrine but also the return of divine authority.

Through repentance, desire, humility, and spiritual preparation, the Lord equips ordinary people for extraordinary service. Whether through translated plates, angelic visitations, or simple desires to help, His hand is present. You are part of this Restoration. As you act with faith, the Lord will magnify your efforts and guide your path.

Week 4

Theme: Calling Witnesses and Preparing for the Publication of the Book of Mormon

BIG PICTURE

Revelations Covered: Doctrine and Covenants Sections 14–17

Historical Period: June 1829

This week's study focuses on the Lord's instructions to three members of the Whitmer family—David, John, and Peter Jr.—and His call for three special witnesses to the Book of Mormon. These revelations occur during a time of anticipation and spiritual excitement as the translation nears completion and the Lord prepares individuals for foundational roles in the unfolding Restoration.

By June 1829, Joseph Smith and Oliver Cowdery had temporarily relocated from Harmony, Pennsylvania to the Whitmer home in Fayette, New York. The Whitmers welcomed them with faith and generosity, offering a safe environment where the final pages of the Book of Mormon could be translated. In this spiritually charged atmosphere, several members of the family began seeking the Lord's will regarding their personal callings and contributions. The Lord responded with individual revelations filled with promises, encouragement, and instruction.

The Lord also begins to fulfill a prophecy made centuries earlier: that three witnesses would be called to testify of the truth of the Book of Mormon. This testimony would accompany the published record, serving as a divine confirmation of its truth. Section 17 is the Lord's declaration of that mission. It teaches us the sacred nature of bearing testimony and how spiritual witness is always preceded by faith.

Together, these sections show how the Lord prepares ordinary people for sacred purposes. They also reveal His pattern of calling individuals through revelation, preparing them through obedience, and sustaining them through spiritual gifts. Each revelation reflects the love and trust the Lord extends to those who desire to serve.

Key People:

• Joseph Smith Jr. – Completing the translation and receiving direction for others

• David Whitmer – Aided the translation effort and would become one of the Three Witnesses

• John Whitmer – Sought the Lord's will and was later called to keep Church records

• Peter Whitmer Jr. – Called to serve and support the Lord's work

• Oliver Cowdery and Martin Harris – Along with David Whitmer, called to be the Three Witnesses

Key Locations:

• Fayette, New York – The Whitmer home, where the final translation and these revelations took place

Spiritual Themes:

• The Lord knows us personally and answers individual desires to serve

• Faith is required before spiritual manifestation

• Testimony is a sacred stewardship

• The Lord keeps His promises across generations

• The Book of Mormon is central to the Restoration and is supported by divine witnesses

• The Lord calls ordinary people to do extraordinary things

SPIRITUAL CONTEXT AND OVERVIEW OF THE SECTIONS

Section 14 – Revelation to David Whitmer

David Whitmer had already shown great faith by inviting Joseph and Oliver into his home and assisting with the translation effort. This revelation assures him that his desire to serve is recognized by the Lord and that eternal rewards await those who labor in faith. He is promised that if he endures to the end, he will have the gift of eternal life.

Key Concepts:

• The Lord knows the sincere desires of the heart

• Laboring in the gospel brings eternal rewards

• Endurance is as important as initial zeal

Section 15 – Revelation to John Whitmer

John seeks the Lord's will, and the Lord answers with a brief but personal revelation. He is told that preaching the gospel and calling others to repentance is the most important work he can do. The Lord's message is personal and emphasizes eternal values over worldly ambitions.

Key Concepts:

• The Lord's word is tailored to the individual

• Bringing souls to Christ is the greatest joy

• Small revelations can carry great significance

Section 16 – Revelation to Peter Whitmer Jr.

This revelation is nearly identical to John's, reinforcing the message that each person's mission is known to God. Peter is also called to preach repentance and assured that his service is valuable in the Lord's work.

Key Concepts:

• The Lord speaks to individuals in familiar ways

• Repetition emphasizes importance

• Every contribution in the gospel is sacred

Section 17 – Calling of the Three Witnesses

The Lord declares that Oliver Cowdery, David Whitmer, and Martin Harris will be given the privilege to see the gold plates and bear special witness of the Book of Mormon. This sacred experience will confirm their testimonies and become part of the permanent record accompanying the book.

Key Concepts:

- Witnesses are chosen and prepared by the Lord
- Faith precedes the right to see sacred things
- Testifying is both a blessing and a responsibility
- The Lord fulfills His promises in exact detail

LITTLE PICTURE: SECTION-BY-SECTION INSIGHT

Section 14 – The Lord Recognizes a Willing Heart

This revelation comes to David Whitmer after he has already shown faith by inviting Joseph and Oliver into his family's home, creating a safe haven for the final stages of the Book of Mormon translation. David is eager to know how he can serve more directly in the unfolding work of the Restoration. The Lord responds with a powerful personal message. He reassures David that his desires are known, his efforts are meaningful, and that great blessings—including eternal life—await those who remain faithful.

Before You Read: Reflect on a time when you supported someone else's service or calling. How did that support become part of your own spiritual growth?

Key Verses to Watch:

- Verse 2: "Behold, I am God; give heed unto my word"
- Verse 7: "If you shall ask, you shall receive revelation upon revelation"
- Verse 8: "If you endure to the end you shall have eternal life"

Core Message: The Lord sees the desires of our hearts and promises that those who faithfully serve will receive eternal rewards. Enduring in faith matters just as much as beginning with zeal.

Section 15 – A Personal and Focused Call to John Whitmer

John Whitmer receives a revelation nearly as short as it is powerful. He seeks to know what the Lord would have him do. The answer is direct and uplifting: bringing souls to Christ is the greatest work one can engage in. The Lord acknowledges John's request with affection and focus, reminding him that the joy of sharing the gospel surpasses all worldly achievements. Though brief, this revelation affirms that the Lord speaks personally and powerfully to each individual.

Before You Read: What do you hope the Lord sees in your heart when you ask Him for direction?

Key Verses to Watch:

- Verse 4: "For many times you have desired of me to know that which would be of the most worth unto you"
- Verse 6: "The thing which will be of the most worth unto you will be to declare repentance unto this people"

Core Message: The most worthwhile thing we can do is help others turn to Christ. Even short revelations carry eternal truths when they answer sincere questions.

Section 16 – The Sacredness of Repetition in Peter Whitmer Jr.'s Call

Peter Whitmer Jr. receives a revelation nearly identical to the one his brother John received. At first glance, it might seem repetitive. But the Lord often repeats truths not because He has nothing new to say, but because He wants those truths deeply rooted in our hearts. The message to Peter confirms that he, too, is known and called. His willingness to serve is honored, and his path is affirmed with divine simplicity.

Before You Read: Why do you think the Lord might give similar counsel to different people? What does that tell us about His priorities?

Key Verses to Watch:

- Verse 4: "Declare repentance unto this people, that you may bring souls unto me"
- Verse 6: "Endure to the end, and you shall have eternal life"

Core Message: Repetition is a divine teaching tool. When the Lord gives the same message twice, we should pay close attention. Every individual calling matters to Him.

Section 17 – A Witnessing Assignment Rooted in Faith and Prophecy

This section stands apart as a divine commission. It addresses Oliver Cowdery, David Whitmer, and Martin Harris, declaring that they will be privileged to see the gold plates, the breastplate, the sword of Laban, the Liahona, and the Urim and Thummim. These items are not mere relics but sacred instruments of God's work. The Lord emphasizes that faith must precede this spiritual manifestation. Their witness will go beyond sight—it will be a lifelong responsibility to testify, regardless of opposition.

Before You Read: If the Lord gave you a spiritual experience to share with the world, how would you carry that responsibility?

Key Verses to Watch:

- Verse 1: "It is by your faith that you shall obtain a view of them"
- Verse 3: "It is by my power that you have seen them"
- Verse 5: "You shall testify that you have seen them, even as my servant Joseph Smith, Jun., has seen them"

Core Message: Sacred experiences require preparation and faith. Being a witness of truth is not only a privilege but also a lifelong stewardship.

SPIRITUAL GUIDING QUESTIONS

1. **In Section 14, David Whitmer is promised eternal life if he endures.**
2. **What does "enduring to the end" mean to you personally?**
3. How might that endurance look in your daily life right now?
4. **Sections 15 and 16 emphasize preaching repentance as the most worthwhile work.**
5. **Why do you think the Lord repeated the same message to both John and Peter Whitmer Jr.?**
6. What does that repetition say about your own potential to serve?
7. **In Section 17, the Three Witnesses are told they will see sacred objects because of their faith.**
8. **What relationship do you see between faith and spiritual experiences in your own life?**
9. Have you ever received a witness from the Spirit after exercising faith?
10. **These revelations were given to individuals who sincerely wanted to serve.**
11. **What do these sections teach about how the Lord calls and prepares His servants?**
12. How can you show the Lord that you are willing to be used in His work?

JOURNAL PROMPTS

- Write about a time when your desire to serve led you to a new opportunity.

How did that experience shape your understanding of your role in God's work?

- Record a personal definition of "eternal life" based on what you read in Section 14.

What do you feel inspired to do now in order to endure and qualify for that promise?

- Make a list of ways you can "declare repentance" in simple, everyday moments.

How might a conversation, act of kindness, or quiet example help someone come closer to Christ?

- Reflect on Section 17's description of the Three Witnesses.

What would it feel like to be entrusted with a spiritual testimony for the benefit of others?

How can you strengthen your own witness of the Book of Mormon?

APPLICATION FOR YOUTH AND ADULTS

For Youth:

This week, try to find one way to "bring a soul to Christ," as mentioned in Sections 15 and 16. This doesn't have to be big—it could mean sharing a scripture with a friend, showing kindness, or standing up for your beliefs. At the end of the week, write down how it felt and what you learned.

For Adults:

Take time this week to ponder your spiritual gifts and desires. Write a short prayer or letter to the Lord, offering your heart and asking how you can best serve in His work. Then, act on a prompting—even if it's something small like reaching out to someone, sharing your testimony, or supporting someone else's calling.

CLOSING THOUGHTS FOR WEEK 4

The Lord's voice in these revelations is deeply personal. He speaks to David, John, Peter, Oliver, and Martin not as distant figures, but as trusted friends. He calls them by name, acknowledges their desires, and outlines their spiritual missions with clarity and care.

These sections remind us that the Lord does not wait for perfect people to do His work. He calls the willing, prepares the humble, and magnifies the sincere. The Three Witnesses were not chosen for their flawless record but for their faith, desire, and willingness to testify.

As you reflect on this week's revelations, consider how the Lord might be preparing you. Whether through spiritual nudges, quiet reassurances, or opportunities to serve, He is actively shaping your path. Just like the early Saints, your contribution is needed, your witness is valuable, and your name is known to Him.

Week 5

Theme: The Worth of Souls, Missionary Work, and the Foundation of the Church

BIG PICTURE

Revelations Covered: Doctrine and Covenants Sections 18–20

Historical Period: June 1829 – April 1830

This week's revelations mark a major turning point in the Restoration. After months of translating sacred scripture, the Lord now begins preparing His servants to share the gospel widely and organize His Church on earth once more. These sections are rich in doctrine, purpose, and vision. They emphasize the infinite worth of souls, the depth of Christ's Atonement, and the foundational principles upon which the Church would be built.

Section 18 speaks of the value of individual souls and the sacred responsibility of helping them come unto Christ. The Lord directs Joseph Smith and Oliver Cowdery to begin identifying the Twelve Apostles and commissions them to preach repentance. Martin Harris is called to humility and reminded of his role in helping the Book of Mormon go to the world.

Section 19 continues this focus but with profound urgency. Jesus Christ speaks in the first person, revealing the suffering He endured for humanity and the pain that awaits those who refuse to repent. The section is addressed to Martin Harris, who is wrestling with his fears about sacrificing wealth to publish the Book of Mormon. The Lord tells him to act in faith, promising that his sacrifice will bring eternal blessings.

Section 20, often called the "Articles and Covenants of the Church," was given just before the Church's formal organization on April 6, 1830. It outlines the doctrine of Christ, the roles of priesthood holders, the importance of record-keeping, and the sacred nature of ordinances like baptism and the sacrament. It gives the Church structure, direction, and authority, centered on Christ and His gospel.

These three revelations move the Restoration from private translation to public invitation, from individual inspiration to Church organization. Together, they show how the Lord builds His kingdom—soul by soul, line by line.

Section 18 – The Worth of Souls and the Call to Ministry

Received as the translation of the Book of Mormon neared completion, this revelation instructs Joseph Smith and Oliver Cowdery to prepare for the calling of the Twelve Apostles. The Lord emphasizes the eternal value of every soul and teaches that missionary work is sacred and joyful. He invites Martin Harris to humble himself and assist in the work.

Key Concepts:

• Every soul is "great in the sight of God"

• Preaching repentance is the highest labor

• The calling of the Twelve is divinely guided

• Missionary work is both sacred and joyful

Section 19 – The Atonement, Repentance, and Sacrifice

Jesus Christ speaks directly in this section, describing the agony He experienced for all humanity. The revelation is addressed to Martin Harris, who was hesitant to sell part of his land to fund the Book of Mormon's publication. The Lord urges Martin to act in faith and sacrifice without fear, teaching that repentance spares us from unnecessary suffering.

Key Concepts:

• The Savior's Atonement is real, personal, and powerful

• Repentance is urgent and essential

• Temporal sacrifice can lead to eternal blessings

• Fear and pride must be replaced with obedience and trust

Section 20 – The Constitution of the Restored Church

This revelation was given shortly before the Church's organization. It establishes core doctrines of the gospel, including faith in Jesus Christ, repentance, baptism, and the Holy Ghost. It outlines the duties of priesthood offices, introduces the sacrament prayers, and emphasizes the importance of record keeping and unity. It formalizes the Church's structure and reaffirms that it is built upon Christ's restored gospel.

Key Concepts:

• The Church is founded on the doctrine of Christ

• Priesthood duties and ordinances are clearly defined

• Baptism and sacrament must be performed with authority

• The Church must be organized by divine instruction and sustained by its members

Key People:

• Joseph Smith Jr. – Called to lead, translate, and organize the Church

• Oliver Cowdery – Assigned to help call the Twelve and preach repentance

• Martin Harris – Urged to act in faith and fund the Book of Mormon's publication

Key Locations:

• Fayette, New York – Where the Church was organized and early revelations were received

Spiritual Themes:

• Every soul is of infinite worth

• The Atonement of Jesus Christ is central to God's plan

• True sacrifice brings lasting blessings

• The Church is built upon restored authority, doctrine, and sacred ordinances

• Missionary work is a divinely appointed calling

LITTLE PICTURE: SECTION-BY-SECTION INSIGHT

Section 18 – The Worth of Souls and the Call to Gather Apostles

Section 18 comes as the translation of the Book of Mormon nears its completion. Joseph Smith and Oliver Cowdery seek guidance about what comes next. The Lord responds with a powerful revelation emphasizing the worth of souls and the urgency of building His kingdom. One of the most quoted verses in all of scripture is found here: "Remember the worth of souls is great in the sight of God" (verse 10). This line sets the tone for the Restoration's missionary focus.

The Lord instructs Joseph and Oliver to "build up my church" and to begin searching for the Twelve Apostles, a key step in restoring the ancient pattern of Church governance. Martin Harris is also addressed, urged to repent and assist in the coming work. This section affirms that missionary work is not merely an organizational duty, but a sacred stewardship born out of love for individuals. It also teaches that true leadership begins with repentance, humility, and a desire to bring others to Christ.

Before You Read: Think about the people in your life who may need spiritual support. How can you see them as the Lord sees them?

Key Verses to Watch:

- Verse 10: "Remember the worth of souls is great in the sight of God"
- Verse 15: "If you should labor all your days… and bring, save it be one soul… how great shall be your joy"
- Verse 36: "Wherefore, you can testify that you have heard my voice, and know my words"

Core Message: Souls are priceless. The Lord calls us to seek them with love, guided by personal revelation and willingness to act.

Section 19 – The Voice of Christ and the Depth of the Atonement

This section is unique because the Savior speaks in the first person with powerful intensity and vulnerability. Addressed to Martin Harris, who has hesitated to fully commit to the financial sacrifice required to publish the Book of Mormon, this revelation is part command, part comfort, and part warning. The Lord reveals that He suffered the full weight of human sin so that we might not have to, if we repent. He describes the torment He experienced, emphasizing that His suffering was real, voluntary, and redemptive.

Martin is called to humble himself and "impart a portion of thy property… unto the printing of the Book of Mormon" (verse 34). The Lord promises that this offering will lead to blessings beyond measure. Through this revelation, we learn that our sacrifices for the Lord's work—especially those that cost us something—are consecrated by His Atonement.

Before You Read: Reflect on the Savior's suffering. How does understanding His Atonement affect the way you approach repentance and sacrifice?

Key Verses to Watch:

- Verse 16–18: "I, God, have suffered these things for all… which suffering caused myself, even God… to bleed at every pore"
- Verse 23: "Learn of me… and you shall find rest to your souls"
- Verse 34: "Impart a portion of thy property… to the printing of the Book of Mormon"

Core Message: The Savior's Atonement is deeply personal and incredibly powerful. He invites us to repent, sacrifice willingly, and participate in His redemptive work.

Section 20 – The Founding Document of the Restored Church

Section 20 is often called the "Articles and Covenants" of the Church. It serves as the Lord's constitution for how His Church should be organized, what it should teach, and how it should function. It was received just before the Church's official organization on April 6, 1830.

This lengthy and foundational section includes a sweeping narrative of the Restoration, the basic doctrines of the gospel, and detailed instructions about baptism, priesthood offices, the sacrament, record keeping, and Church membership. It begins by testifying of Jesus Christ as the Son of God and Redeemer of the world. From there, it outlines the qualifications for baptism, the duties of elders, priests, teachers, and deacons, and even provides the exact prayers for the sacrament—prayers still used today.

The heart of Section 20 is this: the Church of Jesus Christ is not a new invention, but a continuation of God's work in ancient times, now restored through modern prophets. Every principle, practice, and ordinance points back to Christ.

Before You Read: Consider what it means to be part of Christ's Church. How does that identity shape your life and purpose?

Key Verses to Watch:

- Verse 17–18: "By these things we know that there is a God in heaven… the Maker of heaven and earth"
- Verse 37: Qualifications for baptism—humility, broken heart, willingness to take Christ's name
- Verse 77 & 79: The sacrament prayers, sacred and unchanged

Core Message: The Church has been restored with divine authority and sacred purpose. Its foundation is Jesus Christ, and its mission is to bring souls to Him through doctrine, ordinances, and community.

SPIRITUAL GUIDING QUESTIONS

1. **Section 18 teaches that "the worth of souls is great in the sight of God."**
2. **How does that truth affect the way you view yourself and others?**
3. In what ways does it change how you think about missionary work?
4. **In Section 19, the Savior describes His suffering in vivid terms.**
5. **Why do you think He chose to reveal these details to Martin Harris—and to us?**
6. What does this section teach you about the personal nature of the Atonement?
7. **Section 20 outlines the foundational doctrines and structure of the Church.**
8. **How do the instructions for baptism and sacrament help you understand your covenants?**
9. What do you learn about Christ's Church through these verses?
10. **These revelations connect personal sacrifice with spiritual blessings.**
11. **How is the Lord asking you to sacrifice right now?**
12. How can you approach that sacrifice with faith and trust?

JOURNAL PROMPTS

• Reflect on someone you know who might feel overlooked or undervalued.

How can you help them feel their worth in God's eyes this week?

• Write about a time when you made a difficult sacrifice for your faith.

How does Section 19 give you new perspective on that experience?

• List the qualifications for baptism found in Section 20, verse 37.

How do these qualities show up in your daily life today?

Is there one you feel prompted to strengthen?

• Record your feelings about being part of the restored Church.

How does it shape your relationship with Jesus Christ?

What responsibilities come with that identity?

APPLICATION FOR YOUTH AND ADULTS

For Youth:

Choose one phrase from the sacrament prayers (Section 20:77 or 79) and focus on it this week. For example: "always remember Him" or "willing to take upon them the name of thy Son." Think about what it means and how you can live it at school, at home, or with friends. Write down one way you acted on it during the week.

For Adults:

Prayerfully review Section 18:15–16 and consider someone in your life who might need an invitation to come closer to Christ. This could be through a kind gesture, a shared scripture, or simply reaching out in love. Plan one action to take this week to "bring a soul" unto the Lord—even if it's just offering hope.

CLOSING THOUGHTS FOR WEEK 5

This week's revelations are both deeply personal and profoundly institutional. They teach that the Restoration is not only about sacred texts or heavenly visitations—it's about people. Individuals. Souls.

The Lord reveals how much each soul matters to Him. Whether it's calling the Twelve, urging Martin Harris to sacrifice for the publication of scripture, or outlining baptismal qualifications, the Savior's message is consistent: "I see you. I need you. I love you."

Through these sections, we watch the Restoration move from translation to proclamation. From spiritual seeking to spiritual structure. And through it all, we are reminded that this is the Savior's Church. It is built on His gospel. And it is carried forward by those willing to labor, testify, and serve.

As you act in faith this week—whether in quiet obedience or bold witness—you are participating in the same work begun in Fayette, New York. The Lord continues to build His Church through ordinary people like you. And through that work, He is still saving souls. One by one.

Week 6

Theme: The Lord's Counsel at the Organization of the Church, Callings, and Courageous Faith

BIG PICTURE

Revelations Covered: Doctrine and Covenants Sections 21–23

Historical Period: April 6, 1830 and the days immediately following

This week's revelations capture the sacred beginning of the restored Church. On April 6, 1830, the Church of Jesus Christ was formally organized in the home of Peter Whitmer Sr. in Fayette, New York. After years of preparation, translation, and quiet testimony, the Restoration entered a new phase: the gospel would now be carried forward through an officially organized body of Saints. These sections reflect the Lord's voice in this defining moment—giving foundational instruction to His prophet, setting doctrinal order, and offering personal guidance to key early members.

The revelations in Sections 21 through 23 provide clarity and direction for the newly established Church. They reveal the balance between institutional structure and individual discipleship. They emphasize prophetic authority, the necessity of proper ordinances, and the Lord's personal relationship with each servant. Though opposition came almost immediately, these early words from the Lord confirmed that the Church would be protected and its mission would move forward with divine power.

Section 21 – Revelation at the Organization of the Church

This revelation was received during the Church's organizational meeting on April 6, 1830. It is directed primarily to Joseph Smith, reaffirming his role as prophet, seer, and revelator. The Lord commands that a record be kept—a crucial instruction that would shape the Church's historical and doctrinal legacy. Members are also instructed to give heed to Joseph's words "as if from mine own mouth, in all patience and faith." This sets a precedent for sustaining prophetic counsel throughout the Church's history.

This section also addresses the coming trials. Joseph is promised strength in the face of sorrow and affliction, and the Saints are assured that if they follow the prophet, "the gates of hell shall not prevail" against them. In this short but weighty revelation, the Lord affirms the spiritual tone, administrative order, and prophetic foundation of the restored Church.

Key Concepts:

• Prophets speak the Lord's words and are to be sustained with faith and patience

• Records must be kept as part of the Restoration

• Afflictions will come, but the Church will prevail through obedience

Section 22 – Clarifying the Need for Authorized Baptism

Section 22 addresses a common question among early converts: if someone had already been baptized in another Christian denomination, was rebaptism necessary? The Lord answers clearly—yes. He explains that baptisms performed without proper priesthood authority are "dead works." While prior faith is acknowledged, true gospel ordinances must be performed by divine authority within His restored Church.

This clarification helped define the nature of the Restoration. It was not a reformation or continuation of existing traditions, but a full and divinely authorized restoration of truth, covenants, and priesthood power.

Key Concepts:

• Baptism must be done by proper authority within the restored Church

• Past baptisms, though sincere, are not sufficient without priesthood keys

• The Restoration reestablishes not only doctrine, but sacred ordinances

Section 23 – Personal Instructions to Early Saints

This section includes five short revelations to five individuals: Oliver Cowdery, Hyrum Smith, Samuel Smith, Joseph Smith Sr., and Joseph Knight Sr. Each man had supported Joseph in the early days of the Restoration, and now the Lord gives them specific instructions. Some are called to preach, others to strengthen the Church or to pray and resist temptation. These short messages show the Lord's awareness of each disciple's heart and their individual spiritual needs.

This section emphasizes that the Restoration was not built on structure alone, but on the faith and testimony of individuals who were known and called by God. The Lord's voice is direct, personal, and encouraging.

Key Concepts:

• The Lord gives personalized guidance to each disciple

• Every member has a role to play in building the Church

• Faithful service, prayer, and testimony strengthen the whole body of Saints

Key People:

• Joseph Smith Jr. – Leading and organizing the restored Church

• Oliver Cowdery, Hyrum Smith, Samuel Smith, Joseph Smith Sr., and Joseph Knight Sr. – Early supporters given individual instructions

Key Location:

• Fayette, New York – Site of the Church's organization and reception of these foundational revelations

Spiritual Themes:

• Prophetic authority is central to the Church's foundation

• Ordinances must be performed by proper authority

• The Lord honors and instructs individual disciples

• Opposition may arise, but the Church will be protected

• The Restoration values both divine order and personal calling

LITTLE PICTURE: SECTION-BY-SECTION INSIGHT

Section 21 – The Prophet's Voice and the Power of Patience and Faith

This revelation was given on April 6, 1830, during the meeting in which the Church of Jesus Christ was officially organized. In front of a small gathering of believers in the Whitmer home, the Lord reaffirmed Joseph Smith's divine calling as a prophet, seer, and revelator. Members were instructed to give heed to his words "as if from mine own mouth," but were also told to do so "in all patience and faith." This balance—of loyalty to prophetic guidance and the personal effort required to follow it—became a key theme in the newly formed Church.

Importantly, the Lord also commanded that a record be kept of all things pertaining to the Church. That instruction laid the foundation for journals, conference reports, minutes, and modern-day Church history efforts. The Lord knew that memory would fade—but written testimony would endure.

He also warned that affliction and opposition would come. Joseph was told that his calling would bring sorrow, but that the Lord would bless him "that he shall be mighty." The Saints were promised protection if they walked in obedience. This section blends the personal with the prophetic: the Church would move forward not by avoiding trials but by facing them with faith.

Before You Read: What does it mean to you to sustain a prophet in "all patience and faith"?

What challenges might the early Saints have faced in doing so?

Key Verses to Watch:

- Verse 1: "A record shall be kept among you"
- Verse 4–5: "For his word ye shall receive… as if from mine own mouth, in all patience and faith"
- Verse 6: "If ye receive these things… the gates of hell shall not prevail against you"

Core Message: The Lord speaks through His chosen prophet. As we follow that voice with faith and patience, we are promised spiritual protection, even amid trials.

Section 22 – Baptism by Authority in the Restored Church

This short but crucial revelation addresses a practical and theological question: Should people who have already been baptized in another Christian church be re-baptized in the newly organized Church of Christ?

The Lord's answer is direct—yes. Previous baptisms performed without divine authority are not sufficient. He calls them "dead works" because they lack the living power of priesthood keys restored through Joseph Smith. The Lord emphasizes that His gospel is new not in message but in authority. This command may have been difficult for some to hear, but it underscored that the Restoration was not a reform—it was a rebirth of Christ's Church, complete with the proper foundation.

Before You Read: Why would rebaptism be necessary, even for sincere believers?

What role does priesthood authority play in making ordinances valid?

Key Verses to Watch:

- Verse 2: "Although a man should be baptized a hundred times it availeth him nothing"
- Verse 4: "I am Alpha and Omega… even so will I fulfill all things which I have appointed unto you"

Core Message: Ordinances must be performed by proper authority. The Restoration restored not just doctrine, but divine power to act in Christ's name.

Section 23 – Personal Revelation for Five Early Disciples

In Section 23, the Lord gives brief but powerful instructions to five individuals who had played key roles in the early Restoration: Oliver Cowdery, Hyrum Smith, Samuel Smith, Joseph Smith Sr., and Joseph Knight Sr.

Each is addressed individually, and though the instructions vary slightly, common themes emerge—testify boldly, pray always, beware of pride, and strengthen the Church. Some are given public responsibilities (like preaching), while others are encouraged in more private discipleship. The Lord's voice here is gentle but firm. He honors their faith and urges them to move forward with courage.

These verses remind us that the Lord sees every heart. He speaks not only to the institution of the Church but to the individual disciple who is trying to follow Him.

Before You Read: What might it have felt like to receive a direct revelation from the Lord?

How does the Lord's personal counsel in these verses inspire your own relationship with Him?

Key Verses to Watch:

- Verse 1 (to Oliver): "Behold, I speak unto you… with a voice to shake the earth"
- Verse 3 (to Hyrum): "Strengthen the church continually… thy tongue shall be loosed"
- Verse 6 (to Joseph Knight Sr.): "Take up your cross, which has been laid upon you"

Core Message: The Lord speaks to individuals. No calling is overlooked, and every act of faith is known to Him.

SPIRITUAL GUIDING QUESTIONS

1. **In Section 21, the Lord commands the Saints to receive Joseph's words as if from His own mouth.**
2. **What does it mean to follow a prophet with "patience and faith"?**
3. How can you apply this counsel when prophetic direction is challenging or unfamiliar?
4. **Section 22 teaches that baptism must be performed by proper authority.**
5. **Why is divine authority important for ordinances to be valid?**
6. How does this understanding affect the way you view your own baptism or covenants?
7. **In Section 23, the Lord speaks individually to five early members. What do these brief personal revelations teach you about how the Lord guides His followers?**
8. Which of their instructions—such as "pray always" or "strengthen the Church"—resonates most with you?
9. **These revelations were given during the first week of the Church's existence.**
10. **What do they show about the Lord's priorities in building His Church?**
11. How do those priorities align with your current efforts to follow Him?

JOURNAL PROMPTS

- Write about a time you felt the Lord speak to you personally—through scripture, prayer, or a prompting.

How does Section 23 help you trust that the Lord sees you and your efforts?

- Reflect on your own baptism. What did it mean to you then, and how has your understanding deepened since?

How does Section 22 affect your gratitude for restored priesthood authority?

- Choose one instruction from Section 21 (e.g., record keeping, following the prophet, or enduring affliction).

Why does this matter today, and how can you live it more fully this week?

- Imagine being in the room when the Church was first organized.

What would that moment have felt like?

What do you think the Lord would say to you personally on a day like that?

APPLICATION FOR YOUTH AND ADULTS

For Youth:

Choose one phrase from Section 23 that you feel applies to you—for example, "pray always," "strengthen the church," or "take up your cross." Make it your focus this week. Write it down and post it somewhere you'll see it. Each day, try to live that instruction in one small way.

For Adults:

Spend time this week studying a recent message from the prophet or apostles. Instead of rushing through, read it with "patience and faith" as taught in Section 21. Note any invitations or principles that speak to you personally. Then, choose one to act on intentionally—either in your family, calling, or community.

CLOSING THOUGHTS FOR WEEK 6

The organization of the Church in April 1830 was a sacred and simple event—but it marked the beginning of something eternal. In these early revelations, we see a Church being shaped not just by structure and meetings, but by revelation, sacrifice, and trust in Jesus Christ.

The Lord's counsel in Sections 21–23 is bold but deeply personal. He does not promise a smooth road, but He promises strength. He does not ask for perfection, but for faith. He invites disciples to receive His word, to serve where they are, and to trust that every soul—every calling, every effort—matters to Him.

As you study and apply these revelations, remember: you are part of the same Church that began in that small farmhouse. The same voice that spoke to Oliver, Hyrum, and Joseph Knight still speaks today. And the same promises of protection, joy, and divine purpose apply to you.

The Church is true. The work is real. And your part in it is essential.

Week 7

Theme: Comfort in Trials, Personal Commandments, and the Power of Unity in the Gospel

BIG PICTURE

Revelations Covered: Doctrine and Covenants Sections 24–26

Historical Period: Summer 1830

This week's revelations capture the emotional and spiritual landscape of the summer following the Church's organization. After the joy of seeing the gospel restored and the Church formally established, Joseph Smith and the early Saints faced swift and intense opposition. Just months into the Restoration's public phase, persecution, ridicule, and legal threats began to mount. These challenges were not abstract—they were deeply personal, and they came quickly.

Sections 24 through 26 are the Lord's response to those trials. These revelations were given not only to guide but to comfort. They demonstrate the Lord's awareness of individual suffering and His willingness to offer reassurance in times of fear and uncertainty. At the same time, these sections are filled with direction. The Lord doesn't simply tell His servants to endure—He tells them how to endure, what to prioritize, and how to move forward with faith and unity.

Section 24 is addressed primarily to Joseph Smith and Oliver Cowdery. At this point, Joseph had already endured false arrests, mocking newspapers, and even physical threats. In this revelation, the Lord speaks directly to Joseph's fears. He reminds him that affliction is part of his calling but that he will be strengthened and protected. The Lord reaffirms Joseph's prophetic authority and urges him to continue declaring the gospel boldly. Joseph is told he is not to rely on temporal labor for his support—his calling is full-time, and he is to dedicate himself to the ministry.

For Oliver Cowdery, the Lord offers encouragement in his calling as a missionary and scribe. Though Oliver had once been promised the ability to translate, the Lord clarifies that his strength is in writing and preaching. This redirection is not a demotion—it is a personalized reminder that spiritual gifts vary, and each has divine purpose.

This section reminds all disciples that trials do not mean failure. Even the Lord's chosen servants are not immune to suffering. But the Lord offers strength, purpose, and clarity in the midst of those struggles.

Section 25 shifts focus in a unique and tender way. It is a revelation addressed to Emma Smith—one of the only sections in the Doctrine and Covenants directed entirely to a woman. Emma had endured much already: the death of children, public scorn, and the demands of supporting Joseph during intense spiritual labor. Now, the Lord speaks to her directly.

In this revelation, the Lord calls Emma a "daughter of God" and assigns her specific roles within the Restoration. She is to comfort her husband, collect sacred hymns, and use her musical and spiritual gifts to strengthen the Saints. Emma is told to "lay aside the things of this world" and to cleave unto her covenants. The Lord reminds her that her "elect" status comes not from position but from faithfulness.

Section 25 teaches that women play vital and inspired roles in the Lord's work. It affirms the spiritual equality of men and women and highlights the personal ways the Lord calls and supports His daughters. Through Emma's revelation, the Lord gently teaches that discipleship may include sacrifice and sorrow, but also song, support, and spiritual power.

Section 26, though brief, addresses the principle of Church unity and the importance of common consent. Joseph, Oliver, and John Whitmer are told to study the scriptures, preach the gospel, and make decisions with mutual agreement. This reinforces the principle that revelation often comes through shared spiritual efforts and that unity is not just ideal—it is essential.

This section also includes the Lord's instruction to "not speak but by consent," a directive that ensures spiritual order and respect within Church governance. These principles would shape the way the Church conducts business, sustains leaders, and operates in councils to this day.

Together, these sections provide a snapshot of the early Restoration in motion. The joy of the Church's founding had given way to the difficulty of discipleship. But in that difficulty, the Lord did not withdraw. Instead, He drew closer offering words of comfort, direction, correction, and purpose.

The trials faced by Joseph, Oliver, and Emma were real. But so were the promises. And so is the pattern: when disciples face hardship, the Lord speaks peace. When roles are unclear, He gives purpose. When unity is fragile, He reinforces the foundation.

As you study this week, consider how these revelations apply to your own moments of stress, confusion, or fatigue. The Lord is aware. He offers strength. And He calls you—as He called them—to declare the gospel, stand firm in faith, and act in unity.

LITTLE PICTURE: SECTION-BY-SECTION INSIGHT

Section 24 – Strength in Trials and the Full-Time Call to Preach

This revelation comes at a moment of hardship. After the Church's organization, Joseph Smith and Oliver Cowdery faced public opposition, lawsuits, and physical danger. Joseph had been arrested multiple times on baseless charges, and mobs were beginning to stir. In this context, the Lord offers reassurance—but He does not promise ease. Instead, He acknowledges the reality of affliction and commands Joseph to continue boldly in his calling.

The Lord tells Joseph that he is "not yet as Job," a reminder that though trials are heavy, they are not without divine purpose. Joseph is to continue preaching, not relying on secular work for support. His ministry is his full-time calling, and the Lord will provide. He is promised protection "for I am with thee" and reminded that his mission is to "declare my gospel with the sound of rejoicing."

Oliver Cowdery also receives direction. Though he once sought the gift to translate, the Lord clarifies that Oliver's strength lies in bearing record and assisting in Church organization. His preaching will bring souls to Christ if he is patient and faithful.

Before You Read: Think about a time when you faced hardship while trying to do what was right.

How do you hope the Lord would respond to your effort?

Key Verses to Watch:

- Verse 8: "Be patient in afflictions, for thou shalt have many"
- Verse 9: "Thou shalt devote all thy service… and in temporal labors thou shalt not have strength"
- Verse 12: "Continue in these things even unto the end"

Core Message: Trials are part of discipleship, not a sign of failure. The Lord strengthens His servants and calls them to continue in their mission, even amid hardship.

Section 25 – A Revelation to Emma Smith

This revelation is unique in the Doctrine and Covenants—addressed entirely to Emma Smith, it provides a glimpse into how the Lord guides, honors, and instructs His daughters. Emma had experienced much sorrow, including the deaths of children and the burden of public ridicule. In this section, the Lord speaks with tenderness and direction.

Emma is called an "elect lady" and given distinct roles: to support her husband, to compile sacred hymns for the Church, and to "expound scriptures" and "exhort the Church." This commissioning shows that women had a significant spiritual role in the early Restoration—not just as supporters, but as leaders, teachers, and contributors to worship.

The command to "lay aside the things of this world" applies not only to Emma but to all disciples seeking to focus on the things of eternity. The Lord reminds her that she will be preserved if she is faithful, and that her inheritance will be eternal joy. Her calling is not ceremonial—it is essential.

Before You Read: What does it mean to be "elect" in the Lord's eyes?

How can personal callings bring comfort and purpose?

Key Verses to Watch:

- Verse 3: "Thou art an elect lady, whom I have called"
- Verse 5: "Murmur not because of the things which thou hast not seen"
- Verse 11: "Make a selection of sacred hymns… to be had in my Church"

Core Message: The Lord sees the efforts and sacrifices of His daughters. He gives them meaningful, inspired callings and supports them with spiritual gifts.

Section 26 – Unity, Consent, and Scripture Study

This short section is given to Joseph Smith, Oliver Cowdery, and John Whitmer. It may be brief, but it lays down key principles that guide Church governance and daily discipleship.

First, the Lord tells them to "study my word," showing that spiritual strength comes through regular scripture study. He also instructs them to preach and to confirm members, showing that even amid opposition, their missionary work must continue.

The Lord introduces a vital administrative principle: all things in the Church "shall be done by common consent." This means that decisions should be made with agreement and unity. The voice of the members matters. Sustaining leaders and making Church decisions are not passive rituals but sacred acts of unity and trust.

Before You Read: What does "common consent" mean to you in a Church setting?

Why is unity so important to spiritual power?

Key Verses to Watch:

- Verse 1: "Study my word which hath gone forth… and also preach"
- Verse 2: "All things shall be done by common consent"

Core Message: The Lord directs His Church through shared decision-making and harmony. Disciples are to study His word, labor in unity, and act with mutual trust.

SPIRITUAL GUIDING QUESTIONS

1. **In Section 24, the Lord tells Joseph to be patient in afflictions.**
2. **What does this reveal about how the Lord views trials?**
3. How can this help you respond to your own challenges?
4. **Section 25 is addressed to Emma Smith and outlines a deeply personal calling.**
5. **How does the Lord's counsel to Emma reflect His understanding of her individual gifts and needs?**
6. What does this teach you about how He sees and guides you?
7. **Section 26 emphasizes unity and "common consent."**
8. **Why do you think the Lord requires decisions in His Church to be made in unity?**
9. How can you contribute to greater unity in your family, ward, or community?
10. **These revelations were given amid early persecution and uncertainty.**
11. What principles in these sections help disciples stay faithful when the path is difficult or unclear?

JOURNAL PROMPTS

• Write about a trial you've recently faced or are currently facing.

How does the Lord's message to Joseph in Section 24 give you strength or perspective?

• Reflect on Emma's calling to compile hymns.

What role has music, especially sacred music, played in your spiritual journey?

• Consider your own spiritual gifts. What do you feel called to do, even if quietly or behind the scenes?

How does Section 25 encourage you to trust that contribution?

• Record your thoughts on "common consent."

What does it mean to you that Church members are invited to sustain leaders and decisions together?

APPLICATION FOR YOUTH AND ADULTS

For Youth:

This week, choose a way to strengthen unity in your home, class, or friend group. That could mean listening more carefully, helping someone feel included, or backing someone up when they're trying to do what's right. Think about what "common consent" looks like in your everyday relationships.

For Adults:

Reflect on one area of your life where affliction or uncertainty has made it hard to keep moving forward. Read Section 24 slowly, looking for phrases that speak to you. Then write down one clear action the Lord is prompting you to take—whether it's to speak, serve, or simply endure with more hope.

CLOSING THOUGHTS FOR WEEK 7

These revelations remind us that the Restoration was never free from hardship. From its earliest days, opposition was real, and sacrifices were demanded. Yet in the midst of that struggle, the Lord gave clarity, purpose, and comfort—not just to Joseph and Oliver, but to Emma, John Whitmer, and the broader Church.

The Lord's words here are personal and specific. He calls by name. He assigns roles. He acknowledges weariness, and He offers peace. He doesn't remove every burden, but He promises His presence.

Emma's revelation in particular shows that every disciple, regardless of visibility, has a voice and a vital part to play. And Section 26 teaches that the Church does not move forward by compulsion, but by consent—by unity, trust, and shared commitment.

This week, as you reflect on your own journey, take courage in knowing that the Lord does not just call prophets and pioneers. He calls you. He equips you. He walks with you through trial and affirms your efforts, however small they may seem. The gospel must still be declared, unity must still be preserved, and the work must still go on—with you in it.

Week 8

Theme: Sacrament Preparation, Apostolic Roles, and Revelation with Order

BIG PICTURE

Revelations Covered: Doctrine and Covenants Sections 27–30

Historical Period: Late Summer – Fall 1830

This week's revelations guide the Saints through growing pains in a time of expansion, clarification, and spiritual anticipation. With the Church now organized, missionary efforts underway, and questions arising about authority and revelation, the Lord provides both comfort and structure. These sections address the sacredness of the sacrament, the callings of early missionaries and apostles, and how personal revelation should operate within the order of the Church.

These sections together teach that preparation—both spiritual and practical—is essential in a growing Church. Whether preparing for sacred ordinances, preaching missions, or leadership roles, the Lord expects order, unity, and personal righteousness.

Key People:

• Joseph Smith Jr. – Presiding over the sacrament, clarifying Church order, and assigning missions

• Oliver Cowdery – Correcting false revelation and leading missionary efforts

• Hiram Page – Mistakenly receiving revelations outside his stewardship

• David, Peter Jr., and John Whitmer – Receiving individual counsel for their missions and spiritual focus

Key Locations:

• Fayette, New York – Headquarters of the Church and site of multiple revelations

• Lamanite Mission Region – The western frontier, including Native American tribes and future Kirtland converts

Spiritual Themes:

• The sacrament is a sacred ordinance with eternal meaning

• The Second Coming is closely tied to our present-day covenant keeping

• Personal revelation is real but must operate within divine order

• Missionary work is a prophetic responsibility, not just a personal passion

• The Lord speaks individually to guide, correct, and encourage His servants

SPIRITUAL CONTEXT AND OVERVIEW OF THE SECTIONS

Section 27 – Revelation on the Sacrament and Future Gathering

While preparing to administer the sacrament, Joseph is told by an angel that any food or drink may be used as long as it is done with a pure heart. The Lord then reveals a future sacrament meeting that will be attended by ancient prophets and leaders. The section ends with a command to put on the whole armor of God to withstand the adversary.

Key Concepts:

• The sacrament is about remembrance and spiritual intent, not the emblems

• A future meeting with Christ and ancient prophets awaits the faithful

• Saints must be spiritually armed against temptation and opposition

Section 28 – Revelation and Church Authority

Hiram Page is receiving revelations through a stone, causing confusion. The Lord affirms that only the prophet can receive revelation for the Church. Oliver Cowdery is asked to correct Hiram gently and teach him the right order.

Key Concepts:

• The prophet is the only one authorized to receive revelation for the Church

• Personal revelation must align with established authority

• Correction should be done with respect and love

Section 29 – The Lamanite Mission and Teaching by Commandment

The Lord calls Oliver Cowdery, Peter Whitmer Jr., Parley P. Pratt, and Ziba Peterson to preach to the Lamanites. He reminds them to teach only what He commands and affirms that their mission fulfills ancient prophecies.

Key Concepts:

• Missionary work fulfills divine promises to ancient peoples

• Preaching must be grounded in revelation

• The gospel message is divinely directed, not self-initiated

Section 30 – Personal Counsel to the Whitmer Brothers

David, Peter Jr., and John Whitmer receive individual guidance. David is rebuked for fears and desires that distracted him. Peter is assigned to accompany Oliver on the mission. John is called to labor and warned against pride.

Key Concepts:

• The Lord gives personal counsel to strengthen disciples

• Fear and distraction weaken service; humility sustains it

• Every disciple has a unique calling with divine direction

LITTLE PICTURE: SECTION-BY-SECTION INSIGHT

Section 27 – A New Perspective on the Sacrament and Spiritual Armor

As Joseph Smith prepared to administer the sacrament, he was warned of danger and then received a revelation that changed the Saints' understanding of this sacred ordinance. The Lord clarified that what matters is not the specific emblems used, but the purity and intent of the heart. The emphasis shifts from ritual to remembrance.

The Lord then reveals a powerful vision of a future sacrament gathering, where Christ will sit with ancient prophets and modern Saints to break bread again. It connects present obedience with future promises. The section ends with a call to "put on the whole armor of God"—a personal, daily protection against spiritual opposition.

Before You Read: When has worship felt most meaningful to you—was it the setting or your intent?

What parts of the "armor of God" do you feel you wear well, and which need strengthening?

Key Verses to Watch:

• Verse 2: "It mattereth not what ye shall eat or what ye shall drink… if it so be that ye do it with an eye single to my glory"

• Verse 5: "A great and last sacrament… where I shall partake with the sons of Levi"

• Verse 15: "Take upon you my whole armor, that ye may be able to withstand the evil day"

Core Message: Ordinances matter because of what they point to. Worship rooted in remembrance and personal righteousness prepares us for eternal covenants and protection.

Section 28 – Revelation, Order, and Church Authority

Hiram Page had begun receiving revelations through a seer stone, causing confusion among Church members. In this revelation, the Lord affirms that only the prophet, Joseph Smith, is authorized to receive revelation for the entire Church. While personal inspiration is real, it must remain within divinely appointed bounds.

Oliver Cowdery is tasked with correcting Hiram—not by condemning, but by teaching. This moment becomes foundational in understanding how the Lord governs His Church and how revelation must align with order, unity, and stewardship.

Before You Read: Why do you think the Lord values structure in spiritual guidance?

How does respecting divine order bring peace to personal inspiration?

Key Verses to Watch:

• Verse 2: "No one shall be appointed to receive commandments and revelations in this church excepting my servant Joseph Smith"

• Verse 11: "Thou shalt not command him who is at thy head"

• Verse 13: "Be obedient unto the things which I shall give unto him"

Core Message: Revelation is sacred and real—but it must function within the Lord's order. Leadership and stewardship are divinely set to preserve unity and truth.

Section 29 – Commanded to Preach and Teach with Power

This section commissions Oliver Cowdery, Peter Whitmer Jr., Parley P. Pratt, and Ziba Peterson to go forth on the Lamanite mission—a monumental step in Church history. The Lord reminds them that their message must be grounded in His commandments and that their mission is part of an ancient promise to restore truth to all peoples.

The section also offers powerful doctrine about the gathering of Israel, the role of agency, and the eventual resurrection. These teachings place their mission in a vast prophetic context and emphasize that the Lord directs every part of His work.

Before You Read: How does knowing your efforts are part of a bigger plan increase your motivation?

What does it mean to "teach by the Spirit and not by the world"?

Key Verses to Watch:

• Verse 7: "Ye are called to bring to pass the gathering of mine elect"

• Verse 10: "The time is soon at hand that I shall come in a cloud with power and great glory"

• Verse 34: "Lift up your hearts and be glad, for I am in your midst"

Core Message: Missionary work is sacred and directed. The Lord sends forth His servants to fulfill prophecy, gather Israel, and prepare the world for His return.

Section 30 – Personal Guidance to the Whitmer Brothers

Each of the Whitmer brothers receives personal counsel tailored to their spiritual struggles and assignments. David is chastised for letting fear and the opinions of others cloud his focus. Peter Jr. is assigned to join the Lamanite mission. John is called to labor and reminded to beware of pride.

The Lord speaks with clarity and care—correcting when needed, encouraging always. This section shows that even faithful Saints need adjustment. The Lord doesn't give general advice; He gives personal direction.

Before You Read: How do you respond when the Lord corrects you?

What can you learn from how He spoke to each brother differently?

Key Verses to Watch:

• Verse 1: "David, thou hast feared man and hast not relied on me"

• Verse 5: "Peter, take your journey with your brother Oliver"

• Verse 9: "John… your mind has been on the things of the earth more than on the things of me"

Core Message: The Lord sees each disciple's heart and gives personalized direction. Correction is part of love. Mission is part of growth.

SPIRITUAL GUIDING QUESTIONS

1. **In Section 27, the Lord teaches that the sacrament is about spiritual focus rather than physical emblems. How does this change the way you think about the sacrament?**
2. What can you do to approach it more meaningfully each week?
3. **Section 28 emphasizes proper channels for revelation.**
4. **How can you discern whether inspiration you receive is for you personally, or something that should be brought to priesthood leadership?**
5. Why is respecting the Lord's order a protection?
6. **Section 29 places missionary work within the context of gathering Israel and fulfilling prophecy. How does knowing you are part of that eternal plan change how you view your efforts to share the gospel?**
7. What can you do to bring greater Spirit-led intention into your missionary moments?
8. **In Section 30, each Whitmer brother receives unique counsel from the Lord. How does this show the Lord's understanding of individual hearts?**
9. When has the Lord corrected or redirected you personally—and how did that shape your path?

JOURNAL PROMPTS

• Reflect on your sacrament experience this past week.

What was on your mind during the ordinance?

What could you do next time to "remember Him" more fully?

• Write about a time when you received a spiritual prompting.

What did you do with it?

How does Section 28 help you evaluate the purpose and audience of your inspiration?

• Make a list of people in your life who might be open to hearing about your faith.

What would it look like to reach out in a Spirit-led, personal way this week?

• Choose one of the Whitmer brothers from Section 30.

How do you relate to his strengths or struggles?

What lesson from his counsel could apply to your own spiritual development?

APPLICATION FOR YOUTH AND ADULTS

For Youth:

This week, focus on one piece of "spiritual armor" from Section 27 (like faith, truth, or prayer). Write it on a sticky note or in your phone and look for ways to apply it each day. For example, if you choose "shield of faith," try using faith to overcome doubts or discouragement. At the end of the week, write a few sentences about what you learned.

For Adults:

Select one verse from Section 29 or 30 that stands out to you. Use it as a prayer focus throughout the week—read it slowly each morning, and ask the Lord how it applies to your personal ministry or calling. Then, act on any promptings or impressions that come as you ponder that verse.

CLOSING THOUGHTS FOR WEEK 8

These revelations reflect the growing and stretching of a young Church—but also of individual disciples learning to live with purpose and order. The Lord was not just calling missionaries or organizing councils; He was teaching how to listen, how to correct with love, and how to build His kingdom with clean hands and focused hearts.

Whether correcting Hiram Page or encouraging the Whitmers, the Lord's voice is firm but filled with care. He values personal revelation but places it within a framework of divine stewardship. He welcomes disciples to His table but reminds them to come clothed in remembrance and righteousness. And He sends missionaries not only with a message, but with power and prophecy behind them.

This week, remember: the Lord still calls, still corrects, and still gathers. The sacrament you take, the Spirit you feel, the callings you fulfill, and the people you serve are all part of something eternal. The gospel is personal—but it's never isolated. You are part of His Church, His mission, and His promised return. Prepare accordingly—with order, reverence, and a willing heart.

Week 9

Theme: Revelation for Missionaries, Counsel to New Converts, and Obedience in Discipleship

BIG PICTURE

Revelations Covered: Doctrine and Covenants Sections 31–34

Historical Period: Fall 1830

These revelations reflect a pivotal time in the early Church when missionary efforts were rapidly expanding and new converts were stepping into discipleship. Each section in this week's study is given to a specific individual, offering personalized guidance and divine encouragement. Together, these revelations reveal how the Lord works with new believers, strengthens individual testimonies, and sends out missionaries to proclaim His gospel.

The context is dynamic: several men are newly converted and eager to serve, while the Church is growing and stretching its influence westward. In these early months, missionary service was both urgent and demanding. The Lord's counsel to each person is tailored, yet common themes emerge—obedience, courage, family responsibilities, and the power of declaring His word.

Section 31 – Revelation to Thomas B. Marsh

Thomas B. Marsh was among the earliest converts and had a strong desire to serve. However, he also had family concerns, especially regarding his wife and children. The Lord acknowledges both his faith and his worries. He assures Thomas that his family will be blessed as he serves faithfully and promises healing and conversion for his household. The Lord also calls him to lift up his heart and preach the gospel with faith and confidence.

Key Concepts:

• The Lord knows personal fears and honors righteous desires

• Family responsibilities are not forgotten in missionary work

• Obedience leads to both personal peace and family blessings

• Sharing the gospel brings healing and joy

Section 32 – Mission Call to the Lamanites

This short but significant section calls Parley P. Pratt and Ziba Peterson to join Oliver Cowdery and Peter Whitmer Jr. on the mission to the Lamanites. The Lord commands them to open their mouths and not fear. He promises to go before them and prepare hearts to receive their message. This mission would lead them not only to Native American tribes but to the future center of Church growth in Kirtland, Ohio.

Key Concepts:

• Missionary calls are divinely appointed

• The Lord prepares hearts ahead of the message

• Fear is replaced by divine companionship and power

• Preaching is not optional—it is a calling and a blessing

Section 33 – Revelation to Ezra Thayre and Northrop Sweet

These two men had been baptized only recently and were now eager to serve. The Lord speaks to them using familiar scriptural imagery, calling them to "open your mouths and spare not." He reminds them that the field is white and ready for harvest and that the gospel message must go forward with urgency. This revelation also introduces the phrase "the Church is coming forth out of the wilderness," evoking imagery of spiritual renewal and restoration.

Key Concepts:

• Even new converts can be called to labor

• The urgency of the gospel requires boldness and obedience

• The Restoration is active and ongoing

• The Lord's voice is consistent across dispensations

Section 34 – Revelation to Orson Pratt

At just 19 years old, Orson Pratt receives this revelation through Joseph Smith. The Lord calls him to lift up his voice and testify, promising great joy and eternal blessings. Though young and inexperienced, Orson is told that if he listens to the Spirit, he will be given words and power. This marks the beginning of a lifelong ministry that would influence thousands.

Key Concepts:

• Age is not a barrier to spiritual responsibility

• The Spirit provides words, courage, and direction

• Joy comes from faithful gospel service

• The Lord calls and prepares those who are willing

Key People:

• Thomas B. Marsh – Early convert with family concerns, called to serve

• Parley P. Pratt and Ziba Peterson – Sent on a historic mission to the Lamanites

• Ezra Thayre and Northrop Sweet – Newly baptized and quickly called

• Orson Pratt – Young man called to a lifetime of testimony and service

Spiritual Themes:

- The Lord gives personal revelation to guide individual paths
- New converts have powerful roles in the Restoration
- Missionary work requires courage, obedience, and trust
- The gospel is urgent, joyful, and always expanding

LITTLE PICTURE: SECTION-BY-SECTION INSIGHT

Section 31 – Family Promises and a Missionary Call to Thomas B. Marsh

Thomas B. Marsh came with a willing heart but worried mind. He had accepted the restored gospel and wanted to serve, yet he feared for his family's well-being. The Lord meets him in that place—honoring his faith while easing his concerns. Rather than asking him to neglect his home, the Lord promises that if Thomas serves with faith, his family will be healed, strengthened, and ultimately converted.

Thomas is called to preach, to lift up his voice "with all the sound of rejoicing." He is not left to labor alone—the Lord promises to open hearts and go with him. He is also warned to beware of pride and to keep all the Lord's commandments. This balance of encouragement and correction shows how the Lord shapes His servants.

Before You Read: Have you ever struggled to balance spiritual desires with family responsibilities?

How can obedience bless those we love?

Key Verses to Watch:

- Verse 2: "Your family shall live"
- Verse 3: "Lift up your heart and rejoice"
- Verse 13: "Be faithful unto the end, and lo, I am with you"

Core Message: When we put the Lord first, He strengthens our families and magnifies our efforts. Faithful service blesses both the laborer and the loved ones at home.

Section 32 – A Mission to the Lamanites

This brief revelation sends Parley P. Pratt and Ziba Peterson to join a small group on a bold assignment: to preach to the Lamanites. Their journey would ultimately have greater impact than expected, leading to the first major Church growth in Kirtland, Ohio.

The Lord emphasizes urgency and trust. These men are to open their mouths, fear not, and rely on divine guidance. Though the mission is daunting, the promise is clear—He will go before them. The mission is more than travel and teaching; it is history in motion.

Before You Read: What helps you feel ready to speak about your beliefs?

How does knowing the Lord goes before you bring confidence?

Key Verses to Watch:

• Verse 1: "Open your mouths… and they shall be filled"

• Verse 3: "I myself will go with them and be in their midst"

Core Message: Missionary service is powered by trust in God. When the Lord sends, He also prepares the way.

Section 33 – The Field Is White, Even for New Converts

Ezra Thayre and Northrop Sweet are brand new to the Church when they receive this revelation. The Lord doesn't wait until they've had years of experience. He calls them now, testifying that "the field is white already to harvest."

Using language from the Bible, the Lord stirs them to action. They are to cry repentance, build up the Church, and prepare the way for the Second Coming. The phrase "out of the wilderness" captures the Restoration's energy—truth is returning to the world with divine momentum.

Before You Read: Why do you think the Lord calls people who are still learning?

What does it mean that the Church is "coming out of the wilderness"?

Key Verses to Watch:

• Verse 8: "Open your mouths and they shall be filled"

• Verse 10: "Yea, the field is white already to harvest"

• Verse 17: "The Church is coming forth out of the wilderness"

Core Message: Readiness is about willingness, not perfection. The Lord uses even the newly baptized to spread His restored gospel with power.

Section 34 – The Spirit Will Give You Voice

Orson Pratt is only 19 years old when he receives this personal call to preach. Despite his youth and inexperience, the Lord entrusts him with great responsibility. The message is empowering: open your mouth, listen to the Spirit, and you will be filled with power and joy.

The Lord affirms His identity as the Redeemer and declares that the time is short. Orson is invited into a work that is both urgent and eternal. His voice, guided by the Spirit, will help prepare the world for Christ's return.

Before You Read: Do you ever feel too young or unprepared for spiritual responsibility?

How might the Spirit help you speak and serve with confidence?

Key Verses to Watch:

• Verse 1: "Lift up your voice and spare not"

• Verse 6: "The time is soon at hand"

• Verse 10: "I will give him utterance, and it shall be given him by the Comforter"

Core Message: The Lord does not wait for perfection. He empowers the humble and the young, giving them voice, vision, and joy in their discipleship.

SPIRITUAL GUIDING QUESTIONS

1. **In Section 31, the Lord assures Thomas B. Marsh that his family will be blessed if he serves faithfully. How does this promise speak to your own desire to serve while caring for those you love?**
2. What sacrifices might the Lord be asking you to make in faith?
3. **Section 32 shows that the Lord sends missionaries with both purpose and preparation.**
4. **How does knowing that the Lord "goes before you" change your approach to missionary opportunities or spiritual conversations?**
5. When have you seen the Lord prepare a heart—either your own or someone else's?
6. **In Section 33, newly baptized converts are called to labor in the harvest.**
7. **What does this teach you about readiness and worthiness in the Lord's work?**
8. Why might the Lord prefer urgency and effort over long experience?
9. **In Section 34, Orson Pratt is called at just 19 years old to declare the gospel.**
10. **What fears or limitations do you sometimes place on yourself when it comes to speaking for the Lord?**
11. How can the promise of spiritual utterance help you overcome hesitation?

JOURNAL PROMPTS

• Reflect on your current responsibilities at home and in your personal discipleship.

Is there a way the Lord is calling you to serve—even if it requires sacrifice or trust?

• Think about someone who helped you come closer to Christ. Were they new to the faith or experienced?

How does their example encourage you to speak up now?

• Make a list of spiritual gifts or experiences you feel the Lord has given you.

How might you "open your mouth" to use those gifts this week?

• Write a short letter to your younger self or to someone younger than you, based on the Lord's message to Orson Pratt.

What truth or encouragement would you share?

APPLICATION FOR YOUTH AND ADULTS

For Youth:

Choose a gospel topic or scripture that inspires you. Study it throughout the week, and then look for a chance to share something you've learned with a family member, friend, or Church group. You don't need to teach a full lesson—just speak sincerely. Remember the promise: "open your mouth, and it shall be filled."

For Adults:

Take a few minutes to prayerfully ask the Lord whom He has "prepared" for you to speak to. It could be someone in your family, a friend, or even a stranger. Write down one action step you can take this week to be a more intentional missionary—whether through testimony, service, or invitation.

CLOSING THOUGHTS FOR WEEK 9

This week's revelations are deeply personal. The Lord doesn't issue blanket statements—He speaks to each soul by name, calling them according to their faith, situation, and capacity. Whether to a young man like Orson Pratt, a new convert like Ezra Thayre, or a family-minded disciple like Thomas Marsh, His invitations are specific, empowering, and filled with love.

The Lord makes it clear: you don't need to be seasoned, perfect, or fully prepared to be called. What matters is willingness, humility, and trust. His servants are not made strong before the calling—they are made strong through it. When He sends, He goes with you. When you speak by His Spirit, your words become part of a much bigger plan.

The gospel is urgent, joyful, and alive. And the Lord is still calling ordinary people to extraordinary work. Whether you're 19 or 90, newly baptized or long-time faithful, the harvest is ready—and so are you. Open your mouth. Lift up your heart. Rejoice. The Lord is with you.

Week 10

Theme: The Calling of Sidney Rigdon, the Gathering of Israel, and Commandments for Church Governance

BIG PICTURE

Revelations Covered: Doctrine and Covenants Sections 35–38

Historical Period: December 1830 – January 1831

This week's revelations mark a critical moment of expansion and instruction in the early Church. As 1830 drew to a close, the Lord prepared the Saints for a major shift—both spiritually and physically. He began calling influential new leaders, emphasized the gathering of Israel as a central purpose of the Restoration, and provided clear commandments for how the Church was to be governed in unity.

Each section in this week's study builds on the growing momentum of the Restoration. More converts were joining the Church, new revelation was being given, and the Saints were preparing to relocate from New York to Ohio. With these developments came the need for increased spiritual maturity, obedience, and organization.

Section 35 is addressed to Sidney Rigdon, a recent convert who had formerly been a well-known Campbellite preacher. He had baptized many into his former church and brought spiritual influence with him into the Restoration. In this revelation, the Lord calls Sidney to be Joseph Smith's scribe for the translation of the Bible and to serve as a witness and preacher of the gospel. The Lord affirms Joseph's prophetic authority, reminding Sidney and others that Joseph was called and prepared by divine means, and that revelation comes through him.

This section emphasizes that the Lord works through chosen servants—even when they are young or inexperienced. Joseph is again affirmed as the one through whom the Lord's word will go forth. Sidney, though a powerful speaker and respected religious figure, is reminded that his role is to assist, not to direct. This moment sets a pattern for Church governance: spiritual gifts are valued, but the Lord speaks through His prophet.

Section 36 is a short but powerful revelation to Edward Partridge, another recent convert who would go on to play a key role in Church history. The Lord praises Edward's sincerity and calls him to preach the gospel, promising him the Holy Ghost and great blessings. This section reveals how the Lord chooses and prepares leaders who are humble, willing, and pure in heart.

Section 37 is the Lord's first commandment for the Saints to begin gathering. He instructs Joseph and Sidney to stop their translation work and focus on directing the members in New York to move to Ohio. This shift would create a new center of strength for the Church and fulfill ancient prophecies about the gathering of Israel in the last days.

This commandment also signals that the Restoration is not merely a spiritual movement, but a physical one. The Lord is calling His people to come together in unity—not only to hear His word, but to build His kingdom in preparation for greater outpourings of revelation and power.

Section 38 builds on that instruction and provides comfort, encouragement, and warning. The Lord tells the Saints that He sees what they cannot see—that enemies are plotting against them and that spiritual protection will come through obedience to His command to gather. He reminds them that He created the world, that all things are in His hands, and that He is their advocate and deliverer.

The section also contains early principles of Church governance. The Saints are told to be united, to care for the poor and needy, and to act in righteousness toward one another. The Lord promises that they will be endowed with power from on high if they follow His commandments. The themes of gathering, preparation, and mutual care become central to the Lord's instructions going forward.

Section 35 – The Calling of Sidney Rigdon

Sidney Rigdon is called to be Joseph's scribe and a witness of the gospel. The Lord affirms Joseph Smith's prophetic calling and clarifies that revelation will continue to come through him. Sidney is to use his talents to support the work, not to guide it.

Key Concepts:

• The Lord calls individuals to support His prophet

• Spiritual gifts must align with revealed authority

• Revelation is centered in the prophetic calling

Section 36 – Revelation to Edward Partridge

Edward Partridge is recognized for his sincere heart and is called to preach the gospel. He is promised the Holy Ghost and joy in faithful service.

Key Concepts:

• The Lord sees the sincerity of the heart

• Faithful service brings spiritual gifts

• Humble leadership is a foundation of the Restoration

Section 37 – First Command to Gather to Ohio

The Lord instructs Joseph and Sidney to pause their work of translation and command the Church in New York to move to Ohio. The gathering has begun.

Key Concepts:

• Obedience requires sacrifice and movement

• The Lord gathers His people for protection and instruction

• Unity precedes spiritual growth

Section 38 – Comfort and Commandment to the Saints

The Lord warns of unseen enemies and offers promises of power and peace. He reaffirms His identity as the Creator and invites the Saints to care for one another, prepare for greater things, and obey His command to gather.

Key Concepts:

- The Lord sees what we cannot see
- Obedience brings protection and future power
- Unity, charity, and faith prepare the Church for growth

Key People:

- Joseph Smith Jr. – Confirmed as the Lord's prophet and seer
- Sidney Rigdon – Called to assist Joseph and preach the gospel
- Edward Partridge – Called as a humble leader with spiritual gifts

Spiritual Themes:

- The Lord speaks through prophets and appoints helpers
- The gathering of Israel is physical, spiritual, and ongoing
- Church governance must follow divine order, care for the needy, and prepare for power from on high
- The Lord protects and prepares His people as they obey in faith

LITTLE PICTURE: SECTION-BY-SECTION INSIGHT

Section 35 – Sidney Rigdon and the Role of Prophets and Witnesses

Sidney Rigdon was a powerful preacher and new convert, bringing influence and enthusiasm into the Restoration. In this revelation, the Lord calls Sidney to be a scribe for Joseph Smith in the translation of the Bible and a witness of the gospel. Despite Sidney's prior religious experience, the Lord affirms that revelation will come through Joseph, His appointed prophet.

Sidney is reminded that the work is not his to direct, but to support. The Lord emphasizes the importance of prophetic authority and teaches that even those with great talent are to labor within the order He establishes.

Before You Read: Why does the Lord emphasize prophetic authority even to spiritual leaders?

How do spiritual gifts best support the work of God?

Key Verses to Watch:

- Verse 3: "Thou didst preach… with great power"
- Verse 18: "I have lifted thee up out of thine afflictions… to be my scribe"
- Verse 20: "My word shall go forth… through the mouth of my servants"

Core Message: The Lord chooses prophets to speak for Him. Others are called to sustain and assist, ensuring the work continues with power and divine order.

Section 36 – A Humble Call to Edward Partridge

Edward Partridge had recently embraced the gospel after careful consideration. The Lord acknowledges his sincerity and calls him to preach the gospel, promising that he will be filled with the Holy Ghost and be blessed in his labors.

Though short, this revelation reveals how the Lord sees beyond public image and into the heart. It highlights the type of leaders He calls—humble, teachable, and ready to serve.

Before You Read: What does it mean for the Lord to "know your heart"?

How can humility shape your willingness to serve?

Key Verses to Watch:

• Verse 1: "I am Jesus Christ… and thou art called to preach"

• Verse 2: "Blessed is this man, and blessed are his eyes"

• Verse 3: "I will lay my hand upon you by the hand of my servant"

Core Message: The Lord honors sincere hearts and calls humble leaders to carry forth His gospel with spiritual power.

Section 37 – The First Call to Gather

This revelation marks a turning point: the Saints are commanded to gather in Ohio. Joseph and Sidney are told to pause their translation work and prepare the Church in New York to relocate.

The gathering isn't just about geography. It's about creating a spiritual center, a place where Saints can be taught, protected, and unified. This call demands faith, sacrifice, and a shared vision of what lies ahead.

Before You Read: How would you feel being asked to leave your home for spiritual purposes?

What does gathering mean beyond physically coming together?

Key Verses to Watch:

• Verse 1: "Behold, I say unto you… that you shall go to the Ohio"

• Verse 2: "Strengthen up the Church… and prepare them for the commandment"

• Verse 4: "Ye cannot serve me where ye now are"

Core Message: When the Lord gathers His people, it requires trust, movement, and sacrifice. But it also brings unity, protection, and new blessings.

Section 38 – A Warning, a Promise, and a Vision of Unity

As the Saints prepare to move forward, the Lord offers both reassurance and warning. He sees what they cannot—opposition and danger ahead. But He also promises protection, peace, and future power for those who obey.

The Lord calls for unity and care among the Saints. He commands them to look after the poor, seek righteousness, and prepare for greater spiritual endowment. The message is clear: the time is urgent, the work is great, and the blessings will come if they walk forward in faith together.

Before You Read: Why does the Lord sometimes ask us to act before we understand fully?

How can you contribute to unity in your faith community?

Key Verses to Watch:

• Verse 7: "I say unto you, be one; and if ye are not one ye are not mine"

• Verse 9: "I will be merciful unto your weakness"

• Verse 32: "Wherefore, for this cause I gave unto you the commandment that you should go to the Ohio"

Core Message: The Lord prepares His people by gathering them, warning them, and blessing them when they act in unity and faith. Obedience leads to safety, power, and spiritual growth.

SPIRITUAL GUIDING QUESTIONS

1. **In Section 35, Sidney Rigdon is called to assist the prophet, not to lead. How do you think Sidney's prior experience influenced this call?**
2. What does this reveal about the Lord's pattern for preserving prophetic authority in the Church?
3. **Edward Partridge is praised for the sincerity of his heart in Section 36. What does it mean for the Lord to truly "know your heart"?**
4. How might you cultivate more sincerity and humility in your own spiritual life?
5. **In Section 37, the Saints are commanded to gather in Ohio. What might it have felt like to be told to leave everything familiar for a spiritual purpose?**
6. Why is physical gathering often tied to spiritual preparation?
7. **Section 38 shows the Lord warning of unseen dangers and calling for unity. How do you react when you're asked to act in faith without full understanding?**
8. What helps you contribute to unity and trust among fellow disciples?

JOURNAL PROMPTS

• Write about a time when you were called to assist someone rather than lead. How did that experience stretch or humble you?

How does the Lord's direction to Sidney Rigdon apply to your situation?

• Reflect on your heart's desires. Do you feel they align with the Lord's will for you right now?

What would change if you invited the Lord to guide your motives more directly?

• Imagine being part of the Saints who were asked to move to Ohio. What emotions—fear, excitement, confusion—might you have felt?

What have you "moved away from" in your life to follow the Lord?

APPLICATION FOR YOUTH AND ADULTS

For Youth:

Choose one phrase from Section 38 (such as "be one," "care for the poor," or "lift up your hearts") and make it your focus this week. Write it down where you'll see it daily. Each day, look for a small way to live that principle—whether by including someone at school, helping at home, or standing up for someone in need. At the end of the week, journal what you noticed.

For Adults:

Take time this week to consider what "gathering" looks like in your life today. It might mean gathering your family in prayer, participating more actively in Church, or drawing closer to others in your community. Choose one action that brings people together in righteousness. Consider reaching out to someone new or offering support to someone struggling. As you do, reflect on how these small acts fulfill the Lord's pattern of unity.

CLOSING THOUGHTS FOR WEEK 10

The Lord's revelations in this period are both instructional and deeply personal. As the Church faces physical relocation and growing complexity, the Lord steps in with precise direction, loving correction, and powerful reassurance.

Sidney Rigdon is reminded that spiritual strength must work within prophetic order. Edward Partridge is called not for his experience, but for his sincerity. The Saints are asked to leave comfort behind and move toward the unknown, not with fear, but with unity and faith. And through it all, the Lord's message is constant: I am with you. I see what you do not. Obey, gather, and be one.

These revelations remind us that spiritual momentum requires spiritual discipline. The Lord is still gathering. He still protects. He still empowers. But only as we act with humility, unity, and obedience.

This week, listen for the Lord's voice in your stewardship. Strengthen those around you. Prepare to move, spiritually or physically, as He commands. Because in unity, in humility, and in covenant faithfulness, He promises: power will come.

Week 11

Theme: The Law of Consecration, Missionary Work, and Building a Zion People

BIG PICTURE

Revelations Covered: Doctrine and Covenants Sections 39–42

Historical Period: January – February 1831

This week's revelations lay the spiritual and practical foundation for building a Zion people. As the Saints began gathering in Ohio, the Lord revealed new commandments and clarified the principles that would govern His Church in the coming days. These revelations focus on personal preparation for missionary work, receiving the Holy Ghost, and most importantly, the introduction of the law of consecration—a law designed to help the Saints live in unity, eliminate poverty, and prepare for the Second Coming.

Section 39 begins with a personal revelation to James Covill, a former Methodist minister who had covenanted to obey whatever the Lord would command him. The Lord gives him a beautiful and promising revelation, calling him to preach the gospel and promising the Holy Ghost and spiritual strength if he follows through. Unfortunately, Covill would quickly reject the commandment, but this revelation stands as a testimony of the Lord's willingness to guide those who seek truth and the need for commitment when it is offered.

Section 40 is a follow-up to Section 39, given after James Covill turns away from the gospel. The Lord confirms that Covill's fear of the world and rejection of the truth led him to break his covenant. This brief revelation illustrates an important truth in the Restoration: receiving the word is not enough—discipleship requires sacrifice and faith in the face of uncertainty.

Together, these two sections show the tension between invitation and agency. The Lord speaks clearly, offers blessings, and extends callings—but each person must choose whether to follow. Covill's story contrasts with the examples of those who were willing to act, leave behind comforts, and follow the Lord into the unknown.

Section 41 marks a transition point as the Saints began arriving in Ohio. The Lord designates Edward Partridge as the Church's first bishop and gives instruction about spiritual order. He reaffirms Joseph Smith's role as the one to receive revelation for the Church and commands that no one should be appointed to positions unless directed through proper channels. This section prepares the Saints to receive something greater—the law that will help them become a Zion community.

Section 42 is the long-anticipated "law" promised in earlier revelations. Sometimes called the "Law of the Church," it is one of the most foundational sections in the Doctrine and Covenants. In it, the Lord reveals principles that will govern His people in the last days: laws about preaching, healing, caring for the poor, moral behavior, and economic sharing. Most notably, the law of consecration is introduced—a sacred principle by which the Saints are commanded to dedicate their time, talents, and property to the building up of Zion.

The law of consecration is not a political or social program—it is a spiritual covenant. It is rooted in love, equality, and faith. The goal is not simply to relieve poverty but to eliminate selfishness and create a people prepared to live in God's presence. Section 42 invites the Saints to stop living like the world and begin building something entirely new—a society governed by covenant and consecration.

Section 39 – Revelation to James Covill

James Covill is called to accept the restored gospel and preach the word with power. The Lord promises the Holy Ghost, strength, and spiritual joy if he obeys.

Key Concepts:

- The Lord gives clear invitations to those who seek truth
- Faith and action are required to receive the promised blessings
- Missionary work begins with personal conversion

Section 40 – The Fall of James Covill

After rejecting the Lord's call, Covill is condemned for fearing the world more than God. This section reminds us that agency is real and so are the consequences of disobedience.

Key Concepts:

- Discipleship requires courage and commitment
- Fear of the world can block eternal blessings
- The Lord honors agency—even when the choice is tragic

Section 41 – Edward Partridge Called as First Bishop

The Lord gives administrative direction as the Saints gather in Ohio. Edward Partridge is called to serve as bishop, and the Church is reminded to act under prophetic direction.

Key Concepts:

- The Lord organizes His Church through appointed servants
- Spiritual authority must be honored
- Bishops are called to serve and administer temporal matters

Section 42 – The Law of the Church

This is one of the most important revelations in the Doctrine and Covenants. It outlines moral laws, principles of Church governance, missionary conduct, care for the poor, and the law of consecration. The Saints are invited to become a Zion people through obedience and sacrifice.

Key Concepts:

- The law of consecration is a sacred covenant, not a social program
- The Church must care for the poor and needy in righteousness
- A Zion people live in unity, purity, and preparation for Christ's return

Key People:

• James Covill – A preacher who receives a powerful revelation but turns away

• Edward Partridge – The Church's first bishop, called to lead with humility

• Joseph Smith Jr. – Reaffirmed as the sole revelator for the Church

Spiritual Themes:

• Invitation and agency are central to the Lord's work

• Zion requires consecration, sacrifice, and moral discipline

• Church governance must follow divine order

• The Saints are being prepared to build a new society, rooted in covenant living

LITTLE PICTURE: SECTION-BY-SECTION INSIGHT

Section 39 – The Lord Invites, but We Must Act

James Covill, a former Methodist minister, sincerely sought truth and covenanted to obey whatever the Lord would reveal. In response, the Lord gave him a deeply personal revelation. Covill was called to preach the restored gospel and promised the Holy Ghost, spiritual joy, and power. The revelation emphasizes that faith must be followed by action—blessings are real, but conditional.

The Lord praises Covill's initial desire and promises strength, healing, and new direction. But obedience is the key. The revelation shows that those who seek will find—but only if they walk forward with courage.

Before You Read: Have you ever made a spiritual commitment and struggled to follow through?

What helps you move from good intentions to action?

Key Verses to Watch:

• Verse 6: "Arise and be baptized, and wash away your sins"

• Verse 11: "I will lay my hand upon you by the hand of my servant"

• Verse 20: "Go forth… declaring my gospel with the sound of rejoicing"

Core Message: The Lord honors those who seek truth. But seeking must turn into doing if we hope to receive His promised blessings.

Section 40 – A Tragic Turn from Truth

Only days after receiving his revelation, James Covill turned away. This brief section offers a divine explanation: Covill feared the world more than God. The Lord does not condemn inquiry—but He does hold us accountable for what we receive. When Covill rejected the call, he lost the blessings.

This moment is a sobering reminder that truth comes with responsibility. The Lord invites all, but discipleship always requires courage.

Before You Read: Why do people sometimes turn away from spiritual invitations?

How can you guard against the fear of the world?

Key Verses to Watch:

• Verse 1: "He broke my covenant, and it remaineth with me to do with him as seemeth me good"

• Verse 2: "He feared man and trusted not in me"

Core Message: Fear and indecision can cost eternal blessings. Agency is sacred, but it must be used in faith, not fear.

Section 41 – A New Bishop and Order in the Church

As the Saints began gathering in Ohio, the Lord provided needed structure. Edward Partridge, known for his humility and sincerity, was called to be the first bishop of the Church. The Lord also reaffirmed that Joseph Smith alone was authorized to receive revelations for the Church.

This revelation teaches the importance of spiritual authority, administrative calling, and proper channels. It prepares the Church for the greater law to come.

Before You Read: What does it mean to be called to serve, not to lead?

How do you recognize true spiritual authority in action?

Key Verses to Watch:

• Verse 1: "I delight to bless with the greatest of all blessings"

• Verse 9: "Edward Partridge… is like Nathanael of old, in whom there is no guile"

• Verse 11: "Appoint him and ordain him to this calling"

Core Message: The Lord organizes His Church through chosen and humble servants. True leadership is spiritual stewardship, not control.

Section 42 – The Law of Consecration and the Vision of Zion

This foundational revelation introduces what is known as the "Law of the Church." It contains commandments on morality, missionary work, care for the poor, and the law of consecration—a covenant to give all we have to build Zion.

Consecration is not about economics. It's about discipleship, sacrifice, and unity. The Lord is shaping a new people—a Zion people—who care for each other, live with integrity, and prepare for Christ's coming. This law invites Saints to stop living like the world and start living like citizens of heaven.

Before You Read: What would it look like to give everything to God?

How can your talents and resources help build Zion?

Key Verses to Watch:

• Verse 30: "Thou shalt remember the poor, and consecrate of thy properties"

• Verse 42: “Thou shalt not be idle”

• Verse 61: “If thou shalt ask, thou shalt receive revelation upon revelation”

Core Message: The Lord’s law builds Zion. Consecration is not just giving—it’s becoming. Obedience, sacrifice, and unity prepare a people to live with God.

SPIRITUAL GUIDING QUESTIONS

1. What lessons do you learn from James Covill's story in Sections 39–40?

2. Why is it important not just to receive truth, but to act on it immediately?

3. Section 41 emphasizes the Lord's order in organizing His Church.

4. Why does the Lord call specific people to serve in specific ways?

5. How do you sustain those the Lord has called?

6. The law of consecration (Section 42) is introduced not just as a law, but as a spiritual lifestyle.

7. What does it mean to live consecrated today, even without formal stewardship assignments?

8. Section 42 also teaches about caring for the poor and avoiding idleness.

9. How can you balance personal ambition with the Lord's call to community responsibility and service?

JOURNAL PROMPTS

• James Covill received a personal call but chose not to follow it.

Reflect on a time when you felt prompted to do something good but hesitated or held back.

What would it take for you to act with greater courage next time?

• Section 40 teaches that fear of man can outweigh faith in God.

Write about a situation where you chose faith over fear.

What was the result—and how did the Lord strengthen you through it?

• Edward Partridge is described as someone "in whom there is no guile."

What would it look like for you to be known for your spiritual sincerity?

How do you cultivate that kind of character?

• The law of consecration invites us to dedicate our time, talents, and resources to building Zion. Make a list of your unique gifts.

How could you consecrate one of them more fully to God's work this week?

APPLICATION FOR YOUTH AND ADULTS

For Youth:

Choose one commandment or principle from Section 42 (like honesty, helping the poor, or avoiding idleness) and make it your focus for the week. Each day, try to act on that principle in a real way—whether by including someone left out, finishing a task with integrity, or giving time to someone who needs it. At week's end, journal about how it changed your outlook.

For Adults:

Reflect on how you can live the law of consecration more fully in your current circumstances. You may not be asked to give up all possessions, but consider: What time, skills, or resources could you offer to help build Zion in your ward or community? Choose one small but intentional act of consecration this week and write down how it felt to offer it freely.

CLOSING THOUGHTS FOR WEEK 11

The revelations in this week's study invite us into something far bigger than personal conversion—they invite us to build a society centered on Christ. Zion is not just a place; it's a people. And the Lord is shaping that people through revelation, obedience, and sacrifice.

James Covill's story reminds us that spiritual potential must be matched by spiritual courage. The Lord invites, but He does not force. When we fear the world more than God, we forfeit blessings that were within reach.

The call of Edward Partridge and the law of consecration reveal that Zion is built by humble, sincere Saints who act in love, share what they have, and seek the Lord's will daily. It's not about wealth—it's about willingness. It's not about being perfect—it's about being unified and obedient.

This week, remember: the Lord is not just asking you to do good things—He's inviting you to become something new. To live differently. To see others differently. To contribute to something eternal. Zion begins when consecration becomes a way of life.

Week 12

Theme: False Revelation, Church Order, and Instructions to Organize and Protect the Saints

BIG PICTURE

Revelations Covered: Doctrine and Covenants Sections 43–47

Historical Period: February – March 1831

These revelations were received during a critical moment in the early Church as the Saints were newly gathered in Ohio. With new converts arriving and excitement building, confusion also entered the scene. False revelations, competing voices, and spiritual disorder threatened the unity of the Saints. In response, the Lord revealed clear principles to establish order in His Church, reaffirm prophetic authority, and guide the Saints in record-keeping, council organization, and spiritual protection.

Section 43 addresses a specific incident involving a woman who claimed to be receiving revelations for the Church. Though she was sincere, her claims created confusion among the members. In this revelation, the Lord reaffirms that only the prophet—Joseph Smith—is authorized to receive revelation for the whole Church. Others may receive revelation for their own stewardships (such as families or personal decisions), but they may not direct the Church. This revelation marks one of the earliest times the Lord establishes clear boundaries between individual spiritual experience and the structure of Church authority.

The Lord also warns that false revelations can lead to deception and spiritual danger. The Saints are told to gather and teach one another, but to do so by the Spirit and not by personal ambition or competing claims. The Lord's house is a house of order, and that order must be preserved so the Church can grow in strength and safety.

Section 44 shifts the focus toward the public organization of the Church. The Lord instructs Joseph Smith and Sidney Rigdon to call a general conference of the Church. This would be a time for members to gather, strengthen each other, and receive new direction. The revelation also emphasizes that elders are to go out and preach the gospel so that more people can be gathered into the Church. This pattern of preaching and gathering remains at the heart of the Restoration.

The Lord further promises that if the elders teach by the Spirit and seek out the poor and needy, His blessings will attend them. The gospel is not only about doctrine—it is about caring for others and lifting those in need. This principle will echo throughout later revelations as the Saints are prepared to become a Zion people.

Section 45 is one of the most powerful and expansive revelations given to the Saints in this period. It begins with the Lord declaring His identity as the advocate with the Father—the one who pleads for the faithful. He then speaks of signs of the times, the gathering of Israel, and the building up of Zion in preparation for the Second Coming. The Saints are told to be faithful, watchful, and obedient as the last days unfold.

This section offers both sobering prophecy and glorious hope. The Lord warns of tribulations and judgments but promises peace to those who gather and obey. He invites the Saints to prepare for Zion by becoming spiritually ready and by listening to His voice through the prophet. This is not a call to fear—it is a call to focus.

Section 46 shifts again to focus on the administration of Church meetings and the use of spiritual gifts. Some Saints had begun to restrict who could attend meetings, fearing disruption or false spirits. The Lord corrects this: Church meetings should be open to all who seek truth. The Spirit will guide, and spiritual gifts will be distributed according to faith, not status. This revelation affirms that the Lord's power is available to all sincere seekers, and that the Church should be a welcoming and discerning community.

Section 47 ends this sequence of instruction by assigning John Whitmer to serve as the Church's historian and recorder. The Lord emphasizes the importance of keeping records—not only for historical purposes, but so that future generations will know the Lord's work in detail. This commandment establishes a pattern that continues in the Church to this day.

Section 43 – Revelation Against False Revelation

A woman claims to receive revelation for the Church, leading to confusion. The Lord declares that only the prophet may receive revelation for the Church and reaffirms the pattern of divine order.

Key Concepts:

• Revelation for the Church comes only through the prophet

• The Lord's house is a house of order

• Teaching must be guided by the Spirit, not personal ambition

Section 44 – Calling a General Conference

The Lord instructs Joseph and Sidney to gather the Saints in conference and prepare the elders to preach. He also commands care for the poor and promises spiritual outpouring when these principles are honored.

Key Concepts:

• Conferences strengthen and unify the Church

• Elders are to preach by the Spirit

• Caring for the poor invites the Lord's blessing

Section 45 – Signs, Second Coming, and Building Zion

The Lord reveals signs of His coming and invites the Saints to gather, obey, and prepare. He speaks of the destruction of the wicked and the establishment of Zion for the faithful.

Key Concepts:

• The Lord is our advocate and defender

• Zion must be built through obedience and gathering

• The faithful will find peace in the midst of turmoil

Section 46 – Spiritual Gifts and Open Worship

The Saints are instructed to allow all to attend meetings and to seek the gifts of the Spirit. These gifts are given for the benefit of all and are to be used under divine guidance.

Key Concepts:

• Meetings should be inclusive and Spirit-led

• Spiritual gifts are real, diverse, and faith-based

• The Church is strengthened by openness and discernment

Section 47 – John Whitmer Called as Church Historian

John Whitmer is called to keep records of the Church's revelations and events. The Lord emphasizes the sacred importance of documenting His work.

Key Concepts:

• Church history is sacred and must be preserved

• Record-keeping honors the Lord's works and guides future generations

Key People:

• Joseph Smith Jr. – Reaffirmed as the sole revelator for the Church

• Sidney Rigdon – Commanded to preach and assist in Church organization

• John Whitmer – Appointed as the first Church historian

• James and other early Saints – Taught to discern true revelation from false

Spiritual Themes:

• Revelation must follow divine order to protect the Church

• Gathering brings strength, unity, and spiritual preparation

• Zion is built through charity, obedience, and open worship

• Record-keeping and councils preserve the Lord's work and lead His people

LITTLE PICTURE: SECTION-BY-SECTION INSIGHT

Section 43 – Revelation Must Follow God's Order

A woman claiming revelation for the Church sparked confusion among the Saints. In this revelation, the Lord sets the record straight—only the prophet, Joseph Smith, is authorized to receive revelation for the Church. While personal revelation is real and vital, Church-wide guidance must come through the Lord's chosen servant.

The Lord warns that false revelations can lead to deception. Even sincere people can be misled. Saints are encouraged to teach one another and seek the Spirit, but always within the boundaries of established authority. This ensures unity, safety, and spiritual progress.

Before You Read: Have you ever heard spiritual claims that didn't feel right?

How can you tell the difference between personal inspiration and unauthorized guidance?

Key Verses to Watch:

• Verse 2: "There is none other appointed unto you to receive commandments and revelations"

• Verse 6: "Ye shall not receive them, except it be from him"

• Verse 8: "Gather yourselves together… and instruct one another"

Core Message: True revelation for the Church comes only through the Lord's prophet. The Lord's house is governed by order, not chaos.

Section 44 – Gathering in Strength and Service

The Lord commands Joseph Smith and Sidney Rigdon to call a general conference, creating space for Saints to gather, grow, and receive direction. The revelation also charges elders to preach and to care for the poor.

This section highlights the balance between spiritual teaching and physical care. Strengthening the Church doesn't happen in isolation—it happens when Saints come together in obedience and charity.

Before You Read: Why is gathering important for spiritual strength?

How does caring for the poor prepare us for greater blessings?

Key Verses to Watch:

• Verse 2: "As many as the Lord will shall go forth and preach"

• Verse 4: "If ye are faithful… ye shall assemble yourselves together"

• Verse 6: "Be assembled… to organize yourselves, and to prepare for revelations"

Core Message: The Lord blesses those who gather in His name. Conferences bring unity, instruction, and preparation for future light.

Section 45 – Signs of the Times and the Call to Zion

The Lord begins by declaring His role as Advocate and Redeemer, then shifts to reveal signs of the last days. He speaks of tribulation and destruction—but also hope and gathering. The Saints are commanded to prepare to build Zion.

This is a deeply prophetic section. It gives a view of the future while grounding the Saints in present responsibilities. It reminds them that peace comes not from avoiding trial, but from trusting the Savior and acting in obedience.

Before You Read: What brings you peace when the world feels uncertain?

How does knowing Christ is your advocate affect your daily choices?

Key Verses to Watch:

• Verse 3: "I am he who pleadeth your cause before the Father"

• Verse 32: "But my disciples shall stand in holy places"

• Verse 64: "Ye shall have my law… and it shall be a new covenant"

Core Message: The Lord prepares His Saints for the last days through gathering, obedience, and faith in Him. Zion begins with spiritual readiness.

Section 46 – Open Meetings and the Gifts of the Spirit

Some Church members began limiting who could attend meetings, but the Lord corrects this idea. Everyone—believers, seekers, and even skeptics—should be welcomed. The Spirit will guide sincere worship, and spiritual gifts will be poured out on the faithful.

These gifts vary: some speak with tongues, some interpret, some believe, some heal. All are needed. The Saints are reminded that the Spirit divides gifts according to faith, and no one gift is greater than another.

Before You Read: What spiritual gifts have you seen at work in others?

How can you help make your worship space more welcoming?

Key Verses to Watch:

• Verse 3: "Ye are commanded never to cast any one out"

• Verse 11: "To every man is given a gift by the Spirit"

• Verse 26: "All these gifts come from God, for the benefit of the children of God"

Core Message: Spiritual gifts are real, varied, and given to build the Church. The Lord welcomes all who seek Him.

Section 47 – Preserving the Work of God

John Whitmer is called as the Church's historian and recorder. While the task may seem administrative, the Lord places high value on keeping records. Future generations will learn, be strengthened, and see the Lord's hand through these preserved accounts.

Record-keeping becomes an act of discipleship. The Saints are not only living history—they are writing it for others to follow.

Before You Read: Why is it important to remember and record spiritual experiences?

How can you be a witness to the Lord's work in your own life?

Key Verses to Watch:

• Verse 1: "It is expedient in me that my servant John should write and keep a regular history"

• Verse 3: "Let him continue… and he shall be blessed"

Core Message: Keeping sacred records is a commandment and a blessing. Documenting the Lord's work honors the past and prepares the future.

SPIRITUAL GUIDING QUESTIONS

1. **The Lord reaffirms in Section 43 that revelation for the Church must come through the prophet. Why do you think the Lord emphasizes this order?**
2. How does this protect the unity and direction of the Church?
3. **In Section 44, the Saints are invited to gather in conference and care for the poor.**
4. **How does regular gathering help us stay grounded in gospel principles?**
5. Why is caring for the poor consistently tied to spiritual blessings?
6. **Section 45 contains some of the most vivid teachings about the last days. How can we prepare for Christ's return without fear?**
7. What does building Zion look like in everyday life?
8. **Section 46 teaches that Church meetings should be open and Spirit-led.**
9. **How can we make our homes and wards more welcoming to seekers and strangers?**
10. How do you recognize and cultivate your spiritual gifts?

JOURNAL PROMPTS

• Section 43 sets boundaries on who may receive revelation for the Church.

Write about a time when you received personal inspiration.

How did you discern whether it was for your life alone or something to be shared with others?

• List one way you can help "gather" others spiritually this week—through a message, invitation, or act of service.

How might this strengthen your faith community?

• Write about a scripture or teaching that brings you peace during uncertain times.

How can you "stand in holy places" this week—both physically and spiritually?

• What's a spiritual experience you haven't yet written down?

Take time to record it now. Why is it worth remembering?

APPLICATION FOR YOUTH AND ADULTS

For Youth:

Choose one of the spiritual gifts listed in Section 46—like faith, knowledge, kindness, or discernment. Write it down and pray to develop that gift this week. Then look for ways to use it to help someone else, whether in Church, school, or home. At the end of the week, journal about how it went and what you learned about that gift.

For Adults:

Attend or plan a "gathering" this week—whether a family prayer, a ministering visit, a Church meeting, or simply a meal shared in love. Think of it as a space to teach, uplift, and include. As you do, consider how you are helping build Zion by fostering unity and welcoming others into spiritual fellowship.

CLOSING THOUGHTS FOR WEEK 12

This week's revelations show the Lord's steady hand in a time of growth and uncertainty. The Saints were gathering, the Church was expanding, and with that came confusion, disruption, and spiritual risks. The Lord responded not with panic—but with order. With roles. With gifts. With covenants.

He reaffirmed the Prophet's role, called conferences to unify the Saints, issued prophetic warnings to focus them, and reminded them that everyone—young or old, new or experienced—has a role to play in building Zion.

These revelations teach us that the Restoration is not chaotic. It is intentional. The Lord calls us to gather, to organize, to care, and to keep record. Every effort counts. Every person matters. And every faithful step moves us closer to the city of holiness He is preparing—and preparing us for.

Whether you're gathering your family, teaching in your calling, welcoming a new friend to Church, or simply writing in your journal—you are helping preserve and build the Lord's kingdom. Do it with faith. Do it with order. Do it with joy.

Part 3
Gospel Living, Faith, and Application

Faith in Action and Application: Living What We Learn

Faith is more than belief. In the restored gospel, faith is a principle of action and power. It motivates us to move forward even when we don't see the full picture. The revelations in the Doctrine and Covenants repeatedly emphasize that discipleship is not passive. It requires decision, effort, and trust in the Lord's promises. We are not just meant to learn truth—we are meant to live it.

Throughout the Doctrine and Covenants, the Lord invites His people to act in faith: to gather, to preach, to repent, to forgive, to build, and to endure. These invitations always come with blessings, even when the path is difficult. Action builds spiritual strength. When we live the gospel in real, practical ways—by keeping commandments, serving others, studying scripture, and repenting sincerely—we invite the power of Jesus Christ into our lives. That power enables us to change, to grow, and to overcome.

Faith in action doesn't require perfection. It requires consistency. It means doing your best to follow the Savior, especially when the way is unclear. It means choosing righteousness even when it's not easy. The Lord understands our limitations, but He blesses our willingness. As we act in faith, He expands our capacity. We begin to notice small miracles, feel deeper peace, and develop a stronger relationship with Him.

Living what we learn also means applying the gospel in everyday moments. It might look like choosing kindness when others are harsh, choosing honesty when it's inconvenient, or choosing hope when life feels uncertain. These choices, made over time, shape our character and draw us closer to the Savior. The goal is not to simply know the gospel—it is to become more like Christ. And that transformation happens as we consistently act in faith.

Gospel Questions and Answers: Applying Truth to Everyday Life

The gospel of Jesus Christ invites us to ask sincere questions and seek meaningful answers. That process is central to the Doctrine and Covenants. Many of its revelations began with a question—asked in faith by Joseph Smith or other early Saints. In response, the Lord provided personal, clear, and timely direction. This pattern teaches us that questions are not signs of doubt—they are opportunities for revelation.

We all have gospel questions. How do I forgive someone who has hurt me? How can I strengthen my faith? What does it mean to follow Jesus Christ in today's world? How do I make decisions when the answers aren't clear? The scriptures, particularly the Doctrine and Covenants, help us begin to answer these questions. As we search, study, pray, and act, the Spirit helps us apply gospel truths to our lives in real ways.

Sometimes answers come quickly. Other times, they unfold gradually through experience and spiritual effort. The Lord's pattern is to guide us line upon line, precept upon precept. His answers often come through feelings of peace, impressions in the heart and mind, counsel from leaders, or quiet understanding as we study. The key is to keep asking and keep listening.

The Doctrine and Covenants shows that personal questions can lead to powerful revelation—not just for individuals, but for the entire Church. When we ask in faith, the Lord responds in ways that teach, strengthen, and guide. He honors our desire to understand. He wants us to seek truth, because that process draws us closer to Him.

Asking gospel questions should be a daily part of discipleship. What does this scripture mean for me today? How can I apply this principle in my family? What is the Lord trying to teach me in this moment? When we bring our real-life concerns to the Lord and study His words with intent, we begin to see answers all around us. The gospel becomes deeply personal, and our testimony becomes anchored in truth we have discovered for ourselves.

Building a Testimony Through Consistent Scripture Study

A strong testimony does not come all at once. It grows through experience, obedience, and especially through regular interaction with the word of God. The Doctrine and Covenants emphasizes the power of scripture to bring light, direction, and spiritual confidence. Through consistent study, we build our testimony one verse, one prompting, one quiet moment at a time.

Scripture study is not just a habit—it is a spiritual discipline. It trains the mind to recognize truth and tunes the heart to hear the voice of the Lord. As we read and reflect on sacred texts like the Book of Mormon and the Doctrine and Covenants, we begin to understand God's nature, His plan for us, and the covenants He invites us to make. These scriptures are filled with doctrine, guidance, and personal promises. They are not ancient relics. They are modern instruction for today's disciples.

Daily scripture study invites the Holy Ghost. It prepares us to make decisions, strengthens us against temptation, and brings peace in times of uncertainty. It also opens the door to personal revelation. The Spirit often speaks while we study—not just through the words on the page, but through the thoughts and impressions they inspire. That is why seminary, Sunday School, and home-centered learning place such a strong emphasis on daily study. It is how we stay spiritually awake.

Consistency matters more than duration. A few meaningful verses each day, pondered with real intent, can have a deeper impact than a quick, unfocused reading of many chapters. The Lord honors steady effort. Over time, scripture study becomes a source of strength, direction, and joy. It creates a foundation that will sustain faith through life's trials.

For families, shared scripture study can strengthen bonds, open conversations, and teach children how to recognize truth. For individuals, it creates space to connect with God each day. As we develop this habit, our testimony deepens. We begin to feel—not just know—that the scriptures are true. We come to know that Jesus Christ is real, that He speaks to His prophets, and that He will speak to us.

The Doctrine and Covenants reminds us that the Lord's word is "quick and powerful." It is living. It speaks to our time and our challenges. As we build our testimony through consistent scripture study, we become spiritually self-reliant. We stop depending solely on others for answers and begin receiving our own. And that personal witness is the foundation of enduring faith.

Encouraging Youth and Adults to Ask Gospel Questions

One of the most powerful messages in the Doctrine and Covenants is that God welcomes sincere questions. Many of its revelations began with someone asking for understanding—Joseph Smith, Oliver Cowdery, or other early Saints—each coming to the Lord with real concerns. In every case, the Lord responded with clarity, love, and personalized direction. This pattern continues today. Asking gospel questions is not a sign of weak faith; it is a key part of developing strong, personal discipleship.

For youth, questions often arise as they navigate complex social pressures, evolving identities, and spiritual uncertainty. They may wonder how gospel standards apply to their lives or struggle with teachings they don't fully understand. Encouraging them to ask those questions openly—in seminary, Sunday classes, or at home—fosters a culture of faith-seeking rather than fear of doubt. Honest questions can lead to powerful answers when the Spirit is invited into the process.

Adults, too, benefit from asking gospel questions. Whether it's about doctrine, Church history, family roles, or personal challenges, the process of seeking, studying, and listening invites revelation. As adults model this behavior, they show that faith is dynamic, growing, and personal. Questions become opportunities for deeper connection with God, not obstacles to faith.

The Doctrine and Covenants shows us that revelation often begins with a question. When we help others feel safe to ask, we open the door to greater spiritual understanding, confidence, and testimony. Families, teachers, and leaders can foster this environment by welcoming curiosity, studying together, and responding with patience and love.

Applying Teachings in Family Night and Personal Study

The home is the foundation of gospel learning. While Church programs offer valuable instruction, the most consistent opportunities to grow in faith often happen within families and individual study. The Doctrine and Covenants, with its emphasis on direct revelation and lived gospel principles, is especially suited for home-centered learning.

Family night provides a weekly chance to pause, gather, and focus on spiritual connection. When lessons are simple, interactive, and tied to real-life experiences, gospel truths become easier to understand and apply. The Doctrine and Covenants lends itself well to this format. Each section tells a story, teaches a principle, and gives clear direction that can be discussed and applied in a family setting.

Parents can ask questions like: "What would you have done in this situation?" or "How can we apply this verse to our family?" These kinds of conversations help children and teens see that the scriptures are not just ancient words—they're a guide for life today. Even short, sincere discussions can lead to spiritual impressions that stay with children for years.

In personal study, the key is consistency and intention. The Lord promises that those who seek Him diligently will find Him. Daily scripture study, even if brief, opens the door to spiritual growth. When individuals approach the Doctrine and Covenants with prayer and purpose, they receive personal direction, comfort, and insight into their own challenges. Writing impressions, asking gospel questions, and pausing to ponder turns reading into revelation.

Couples, parents, youth, and individuals can all benefit from applying gospel teachings in everyday situations: resolving conflict, making decisions, or serving others. The scriptures offer more than information—they offer transformation. That transformation happens when the gospel becomes something we *do*, not just something we *know*.

The Doctrine and Covenants encourages families to teach their children "to pray, and to walk uprightly before the Lord" (D&C 68:28). When family night and personal study are guided by this spirit, they become tools for strengthening relationships, building testimonies, and inviting the Spirit into the home.

Reflection, Revelation, and Gospel Study

True gospel study is not only about reading—it's about reflecting. The Lord often reveals truth when we take time to ponder, to ask, and to listen. The Doctrine and Covenants teaches that the Lord speaks to both the mind and the heart. That communication grows clearer when we allow space in our study for quiet reflection and spiritual listening.

Revelation is personal. It doesn't always come in grand visions. More often, it arrives as small impressions—peace, clarity, or a recurring thought. When we make time to reflect during our study, we learn to recognize that voice. Instead of rushing through chapters, we begin to ask, "What is the Lord saying to me today?"

Writing in a journal, marking scriptures, and even sitting quietly after reading allows the Spirit to work with us. These small acts create spiritual sensitivity. The more we practice this kind of study, the more we recognize patterns in how the Lord communicates. We come to know His voice in our lives.

Reflection also strengthens faith. As we look back on our studies and see how the Lord answered prayers or confirmed truth, we begin to build spiritual memory. We remember how it felt to receive an answer, how certain verses brought peace, or how a small prompting led to a big decision. This memory becomes part of our testimony.

Gospel study that includes reflection helps us move from knowing about Christ to knowing *Him*. The Doctrine and Covenants is filled with invitations to draw near to the Lord, to seek, to knock, and to hear His voice. Each of these requires more than reading. They require intention, quiet, and a heart open to change.

In classrooms, homes, and personal moments, the power of reflection turns gospel learning into personal revelation. It transforms scripture from words on a page into a conversation with God. As you reflect and act on the truths you study, you invite revelation into your daily life and deepen your relationship with the Savior.

Part 4
Teaching Tools and Religious Education

Ready-to-Use Lesson Plans and Teaching Tips for Youth and Adults

Teaching the gospel can feel overwhelming—but it doesn't have to be. This study guide includes ready-to-use lesson ideas, teaching tips, and adaptable formats for both youth and adult audiences. Whether you're preparing a Sunday lesson, leading a seminary class, or organizing a family discussion, this section helps you focus on what matters most: engaging hearts, inviting the Spirit, and helping learners apply doctrine to real life.

Each section of the Doctrine and Covenants offers powerful stories, principles, and spiritual insights. The key to successful gospel teaching is to start with relevance. Consider beginning your lessons with a question, a relatable scenario, or a short story that connects learners to the principle being taught. For youth, use real-life challenges—peer pressure, technology, identity, or goals—and show how gospel truths offer guidance and strength. For adults, focus on application: how can these scriptures help with parenting, personal revelation, or emotional resilience?

Discussion is central to effective teaching. Ask open-ended questions like "What stands out to you in this verse?" or "How would you explain this to a friend?" Let silence create space for reflection. Invite learners to share personal experiences or moments when the Lord answered their prayers. Authentic stories—especially those shared by peers—can turn abstract teachings into real spiritual anchors.

Each lesson can follow a simple structure:

1. **Prepare**: Study the section ahead of time, identify key principles, and pray for guidance.
2. **Connect**: Begin with a question or story that creates personal relevance.
3. **Teach**: Read verses together, explain key doctrines, and use visual aids or object lessons if needed.
4. **Apply**: Discuss how to live what's been learned. Offer take-home challenges like praying with intent or sharing a scripture with a friend.
5. **Testify**: End with personal testimony and invite others to do the same.

Remember: your goal is not to cover every verse but to inspire meaningful engagement. The best lessons leave space for the Spirit to teach each person individually. Trust that the Lord magnifies your efforts.

Using This Study Guide as a Seminary Manual and Church Curriculum

This guide is more than a companion—it's a flexible teaching tool for use in seminary, youth classes, institute, and adult gospel doctrine settings. Whether you're an experienced teacher or just starting out, the layout of this book helps you create spiritually rich and learner-focused lessons with minimal prep.

Each section of the guide is structured to support the Come, Follow Me model of learning. It integrates key scripture blocks from the Doctrine and Covenants with summaries, spiritual insights, and application questions. Teachers can use the bolded doctrinal points to structure a 30- to 45-minute class, either by following them directly or adapting them to fit the needs of the group.

Seminary teachers will appreciate the consistency this guide offers. Each chapter presents context, scripture highlights, and practical application—all aligned with doctrinal mastery principles. You can assign readings ahead of class, then use the discussion questions to encourage participation. For visual learners, consider drawing timelines, mapping early Church events, or using videos and charts to reinforce the material.

In youth and adult classes, this guide helps move lessons beyond lectures. Each chapter encourages learners to interact with the scriptures through journaling, sharing, and role-playing gospel scenarios. You might invite students to imagine how they would respond to a specific revelation if they were in Joseph Smith's place, or how they would counsel someone facing a similar challenge today.

The flexible structure also allows for hybrid use. Whether you're meeting in person, online, or doing home-centered instruction, the guide offers enough depth for teachers and enough clarity for independent learners. The goal is not to rush through content, but to let each section become a launching point for faith, conversation, and revelation.

Journal Section for Reflection and Religious Education

True gospel learning happens when it moves from the page to the heart—and journaling is one of the most powerful ways to make that happen. This guide includes a dedicated journal section where learners can reflect on what they've studied, write impressions from the Spirit, and track their spiritual progress. Whether you're a teen, adult, or teacher, journaling adds depth, memory, and personal meaning to scripture study.

Each journal prompt in this section is designed to do more than summarize. It asks learners to *think*, *feel*, and *apply*. For example:

- What verse stood out most in your study today, and why?
- When have you felt the Spirit confirm truth while studying the Doctrine and Covenants?
- How can you live the principle of revelation this week?
- What gospel question do you want to ask the Lord? What have you done to seek an answer?

By writing answers to these questions, learners create a personal record of their journey with the Lord. Over time, these pages become a spiritual memory bank. On hard days, you can look back and remember how the Lord has guided you. On quiet days, you can return to past insights and feel inspired again.

This journal section also works well for classroom settings. Teachers can pause during a lesson and invite students to write short reflections. Families can assign one journal question each week during home evening. Leaders can use them in youth conferences or testimony meetings to invite personal introspection.

Importantly, journaling reinforces the principle that revelation is ongoing. Just as Joseph Smith and early Saints recorded the Lord's answers, we too are encouraged to document our own experiences. Even a few quiet sentences written in faith can become a treasured reminder of divine guidance.

Religious education is most effective when it's both doctrinal and devotional. This journal section bridges the two. It supports study, deepens reflection, and helps learners of all ages internalize what they're reading. It turns a gospel class into a gospel experience—one where hearts are touched, voices are heard, and testimonies grow.

Glossary of Gospel and Scripture Terms

Term	Definition
Atonement	The sacrifice Jesus Christ made to overcome sin, death, and suffering. Through it, we can repent, be forgiven, and return to God.
Baptism	A sacred ordinance where a person is immersed in water to show commitment to follow Jesus Christ and join His Church.
Covenant	A sacred promise between God and His children. Made through ordinances like baptism and the temple.
Dispensation	A period when God reveals His gospel to prophets on earth. We live in the final dispensation—the fulness of times.
Doctrine	Eternal, unchanging truths of the gospel, such as faith, repentance, and the nature of God.
Endowment	A temple ordinance providing spiritual power, knowledge, and promises to help us return to God.
Exaltation	Living forever with God and becoming like Him. The highest reward in the plan of salvation, achieved through faithfulness.
Faith	Trust in Jesus Christ that leads to action, obedience, and hope—even without seeing the outcome.
Free Agency	Our God-given ability to choose between right and wrong; also called moral agency.
Gift of the Holy Ghost	The right to have the Holy Ghost as a constant companion, given after baptism through confirmation.
Grace	Divine help and strength from Jesus Christ, especially when we fall short or face trials.
Holy Ghost	The third member of the Godhead. He comforts, teaches truth, warns, and confirms testimony.
Kingdom of God	God's rule and authority in heaven and on earth. The restored Church is part of this kingdom.
Missionary Work	Sharing the gospel and inviting others to come unto Christ.
Ordinance	A sacred, priesthood-performed act such as baptism, confirmation, or the sacrament.
Plan of Salvation	God's plan to help us return to Him. It includes life before earth, mortality, and eternal life.
Prayer	Communicating with God through spoken or silent thoughts to express thanks, ask for help, and seek guidance.
Priesthood	God's authority and power given to worthy men to perform ordinances and lead His Church.
Prophet	A man chosen by God to speak His word, lead His Church, and receive revelation.
Revelation	Communication from God to His children, given through prophets or personal inspiration by the Spirit.
Repentance	Turning from sin and returning to God through sorrow, confession, making things right, and change.

Term	Definition
Resurrection	The reuniting of spirit and body after death into an immortal form, made possible by Christ.
Sacrament	A weekly ordinance of bread and water in remembrance of Christ and to renew baptismal covenants.
Salvation	Being saved from sin and death through Christ. Includes resurrection and, for the faithful, eternal life.
Scripture	Sacred writings from prophets, including the Bible, Book of Mormon, Doctrine and Covenants, and Pearl of Great Price.
Sealing	A temple ordinance that binds families together for eternity.
Second Coming	The future return of Jesus Christ to the earth in glory to reign and complete His work.
Service	Helping others in Christlike love. Strengthens character, fulfills covenants, and builds faith.
Temptation	An enticement to sin or test of faith. Can be overcome through Christ's power and obedience.
Testimony	A personal spiritual witness, confirmed by the Holy Ghost, that gospel truths—especially of Jesus Christ—are true.